JE

SUIS

JACKATAR

Sequel to Back of the Pond
___

Mercedes Benoit-Penney

P.O. Box 22
Aguathuna, NL
A0N 1A0

Email: billpenney47@gmail.com
Telephone: 709-648-9561

JE SUIS JACKATAR – SEQUEL TO BACK OF THE POND

Disclaimer

To the best of my knowledge, all historical entries in this book are factual; all characters, events and incidents are real.

All rights reserved: No part of this work covered by the copyrights hereon may be reproduced in any form or by any means graphic, electronic or mechanical – without the prior written permission of the publisher. Any request for photocopying, recording, taping or information storage and retrieval systems of any part of this book shall be directed in writing to the publisher.

©2021, Mercedes Benoit-Penney
St. Clair Publications

Cover Design: Mercedes Benoit-Penney

ISBN 978-1-947514-45-4

On the front cover the tricolor represents the Motherland of the Acadians. The yellow star, the Stella Maris, is the symbol of the Virgin Mary as well as the Acadian national symbol. Blue represents the Virgin Mary.

JE SUIS JACKATAR – SEQUEL TO BACK OF THE POND

Table of Contents

Table of Contents..3

Dedication..4

Faux Pas..5

Chapter 1: Natural Attraction...6

Chapter 2: John Cabot...21

Chapter 3: Location, Location, Location..37

Chapter 4: Jackatar..54

Chapter 5: Evangeline, A Tale of Acadie 73

Chapter 6: First Families of New-Found-Acadie..89

Chapter 7: Cormack's Expedition...108

Chapter 8: Newcomers Take Root..118

Chapter 9: Hockey...144

Chapter 10: Memories Are Made of This 163

Bibliography...171

Acknowledgements..172

Merci..173

Our Family...174

About the Author..175

Historical, French Culture Association Inc...176

Life's Like That...177

Pictures to Share...178

JE SUIS JACKATAR – SEQUEL TO BACK OF THE POND

Dedication

I wish to dedicate this book to Bill Pilgrim (b. 1938) for his endless days of research on the history and culture of the Southwest Coast. Without his input, I could never have accomplished such an insightful read. As always, it was a pleasure working with Bill and there was never a dull moment. I hope you, the readers, enjoy Je Suis Jackatar, a sequel to the very successful Back of the Pond, as much as my friend Bill and I enjoyed putting it together.

Bill is shown in the above picture doing a presentation against a proposed 'Strait of Belle Isle Fixed Link', just one of a number of causes he has taken on.
(Picture from the Western Star, December 2019 by Frank Gale).

JE SUIS JACKATAR – SEQUEL TO BACK OF THE POND

Faux Pas

Before we delve into the story of our Jackatar friends, I want to send out a heartfelt apology for a huge mistake I made in the original copy of my book, <u>Back of the Pond</u> (Stephenville Pond). On page 60, line 6, I relayed the wrong information on the parents of Ordinary Seaman, Joseph Gallant, P/JX 212476, Royal Navy – Born, October 27, 1919. It should have read Joseph Gallant was the son of "**John Henry Gallant and Elizabeth Bourgeois**". My deepest apologies, for my disrespect, I can only imagine how hurtful and offensive, to the extended family, such a misinformed statement must have been. I thank the many relatives of Joseph Gallant for bringing this mistake to my attention.

Chapter 1

Natural Attraction

A prehistory definition of Newfoundland and Labrador states that 'Human Habitation can be traced back about 9000 years to the people of the Maritime Archaic Tradition.[1] They were gradually displaced by people of the Dorset Culture, the L'nu or Mi'kmaq and finally by the Innu and Inuit in Labrador and the Beothuk on the Island'.

Referring to the above, we can get an approximate timeline as to when the different cultures came to our beautiful Southwest Coast. The recent Newfoundland Indians Culture is slowly revealing itself through the Cowhead, Beaches and Little Passage Complex. A number of sites are being unearthed by archaeologists, here on the Island, such as (1) Cowhead, Northern Peninsula (2) on beaches in Bonavista Bay and (3) in Little Passage, L'Anse à Flamme, on the Southwest Coast, near the community of Gaultois.

---

[1] www. Wikipedia- *Definition of the Prehistory of Newfoundland and Labrador*

JE SUIS JACKATAR – SEQUEL TO BACK OF THE POND

Little Passage Complex

When archaeologists unearthed an Indian site at L'Anse à Flamme, in Little Passage on the South Coast of Newfoundland, in 1979/1980, they found artifacts like arrowheads that they had never seen before. Being only one of its kind, a new name was given to that group, that of Little Passage Complex. These were direct ancestors of the Beothuk.

Beothuk

The Newfoundland and Labrador Heritage site defines Beothuk as 'the Aboriginal peoples of the Island of Newfoundland and Algonquin speaking hunters and gatherers.' They probably numbered less than a thousand at the time of European contact, approximately 500 years ago. They were descendants of a recent Indian Culture called the Little Passage Complex and they lived and hunted in extended family groups. Oral tradition holds that the Mi'kmaq of Newfoundland would undoubtedly have Beothuk blood.

Because of its lucrative resources, the Beothuk were historic visitors to Bay St. George at a time when their numbers were at their peak. They were Indigenous to the Island for centuries, and were seasonal visitors to Bay St. George. We are aware, for example, that they wintered in Red Indian Lake. In spring, among other destinations, such as the Bay of Exploits, they made their way via rivers and ponds to the shores of Bay St. George. Here, they found the sandy beaches easy to traverse. They setup their encampment near St. George's, in a place that is locally known as the Main Gut River. These seafaring people had access to seals, walrus and a variety of fish and wild game.

In addition to this rich resource bounty, they could also reap the benefits from two Basque Whalers (ships) that had foundered nearby in the 1590s. This Utopia would be short lived, for it was also an indication that the arrival of the Europeans was ominous.

JE SUIS JACKATAR – SEQUEL TO BACK OF THE POND

We now believe that during the Middle Ages the Beothuk visited places like Barachois Brook, near St. George's and Point Rosee, (sometimes called Stormy Point), in Codroy Valley. They were probably the first Indigenous to come into contact with the Basque, for Jacques Cartier was known to have come across them when he visited our shores in the 16th Century.

The Beothuk of Newfoundland

The Beothuk were described as being of average height and size, broad shouldered and with rather straight posture. They were generally clean shaven but kept their hair long, occasionally wearing beards. The men and boys were known to have dressed in leggings and loin cloth made from animal skins, tied with a thong and having fringes or piping attached. They dressed scantily in the summer months and were considered, by some, as strikingly impressive.

These Indigenous were thought to be ingenious, intelligent, affectionate, trustworthy and proud peoples and showed great courage in their daily lives. Vengefulness and aggressiveness were not qualities that ruled their lives, but were the exception, when provoked.

Clothing for the Beothuk family was made from caribou, seal or other smaller fur bearing animals, like fox, mink, beaver, marten or a combination of pelts. They all wore leather moccasins, leg skins or ankle boots that had been sewn together, the shape of the foot, but uniquely formed into a cone shaped heel. Fringes or thongs would be added to tie the footwear or to decorate the finished product.

Leggings for everyone sometimes extended up to the waist (i.e. pants). Jackets or coats were made from animal pelts sewn together and wrapped around the body a number of times, kept in place by a homemade belt, which held the inside layer together. If collars, hats or headwear were needed for the colder season they were made for the purpose of being worn with the fur inside, mitts and socks the same. These were often made from the marten which were plentiful to hunt. The clothing was normally tanned, with or without the hair attached. Ponchos were worn, with or without hoods but were mostly worn by women, in which to carry their young. The changing seasons and weather conditions dictated what clothing the Beothuk needed.

Occasionally the whole family wore their hair long and straight, but traditionally the boys and men tied or plaited it back, enhanced with feathers. The women or girls were more likely to braid their hair and add multiple colorful adornments. They often wore jewelry made from animal bones and/or teeth, bird feet, or ivory that was carved in intricate patterns. Such trinkets were added to the edges of their clothing.

All members of the family wore red ochre or red stain from iron rich soil, in order to paint their faces and bodies. They also put grease on their exposed skin which, combined with red ochre, protected them from the sun and flies in the warm months. Their red skin color was an identifiable feature of the Beothuk tribe. Even their new born were initiated into the practice, by receiving their first coat of red ochre which, to them, also had religious connotations.

Did you ever hear the old proverb, 'The road to hell is paved with good intentions, and when acted upon, may have unintended consequences?' By 1829, these noble Indigenous, the Beothuk, so in tune with nature were believed, by many, to have succumbed to the typical good intentions of newcomers. We are told that the Colonial Government of Newfoundland, at that time, realized that the Beothuk were declining in numbers and were now in distress. The decision was made to capture one of the women, with good intentions some say, of establishing friendly relations. She could be returned, later, with gifts and a message of peace and hope for the future. Ironically, when this search party finally encountered a small group of Beothuk and captured a young woman Demasduit, her husband Nonosbawsut was killed coming to her defense. Having just recently given birth to a baby boy, Demasduit, running with her new-born through the snow, realized that she was too late to flee. Pleading for the capturers to spare their lives, she lifted up her shirt to expose her swollen breasts, showing them that she had to be spared, in order to nurse her newborn. In spite of her pleas, Demasduit was captured and her baby was left behind. He died of starvation some days later. Demasduit was captured in 1818, brought to St. John's in the spring of 1819 by Church of England Priest Rev. John Leigh and John Peyton Junior. There, Lady Hamilton, wife of Sir Charles Hamilton (1767– 1849), painted the above portrait.

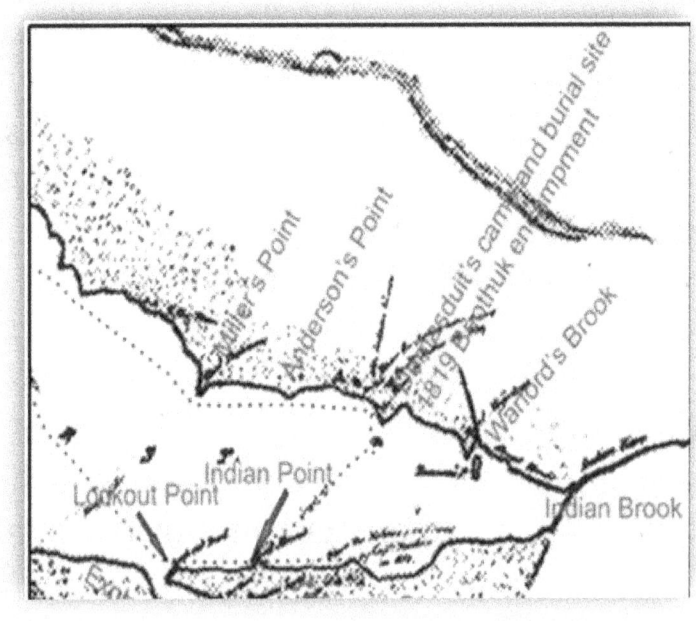

JE SUIS JACKATAR – SEQUEL TO BACK OF THE POND

Beothuk History

W. E. Cormack (1796-1868) had a keen interest in studying, promoting and preserving Beothuk Culture and history. By the 1820s, there were few Beothuk left on the Island. In **1822**, he made at least one trip across the interior, searching for proof of their existence, with no success.

Beothuk Canoe

Taking into consideration the times (1800s), the Europeans looked upon the Beothuk as savages. They lived in the woods, spoke an unfamiliar dialect and led a nomadic existence. Clothing was made of animal skins and they covered their bodies with red ochre. This protection against the flies, gave rise to the term '**Red Skins**' that was used by Europeans to describe all Indigenous peoples of North America. Because the Beothuks were found in the wilds, they were considered more like pagans than Christians, but Alas! They were even treated worse than pagans.

Mamateek type of wigwam used for Beothuk Home

Most of the European settlers were indifferent to the plight of the Beothuk. They disregarded the fact that this ethnic group was there long before them. The European settlers were taking over nature's reserves and ignoring the plight of the original settlers, i.e. Beothuk.

Rivers teeming with salmon were blocked off with the white man's nets. The once plentiful fish, that the Beothuk depended on, now became a lucrative source of income for the British. They filled up their vessels, found a ready market in Europe, Canada and the United States and then returned for more. The English immediately developed a sense of ownership. The Beothuk no longer felt safe near the coastline for fear of being seen, kidnapped or harmed. It was common practice with some captains to kidnap men or boys to work on their fishing vessels, using them for whatever they wished. Crew members were often treated like slaves or forced by press gangs to go on board. It was not uncommon for women to be taken as servants, slaves or worse. These are several good reasons why the Beothuk were driven inland, where food was scarce. In the 1800s, when Newfoundland was still a colony under British rule, the Indigenous peoples were not used to being in close contact with others, not even with the other Indigenous group on the Island, the Mi'kmaq.

There is a story passed down, by oral tradition, about Bossy Paul, (as some nicknamed him), a Mi'kmaw trapper in conflict with a Beothuk woman, Shanawdithit. According to Richard Evans, it took place in Northern Arm, the Bay of Exploits area. There, Bossy Paul had discharged his musket at Shanawdithit, injuring her in the back and leg. It is believed that the person known as Bossy Paul might have been known, by some, as Noel Paul and gotten his nickname Boss or Bossy from the Beothuk, for obvious reasons.

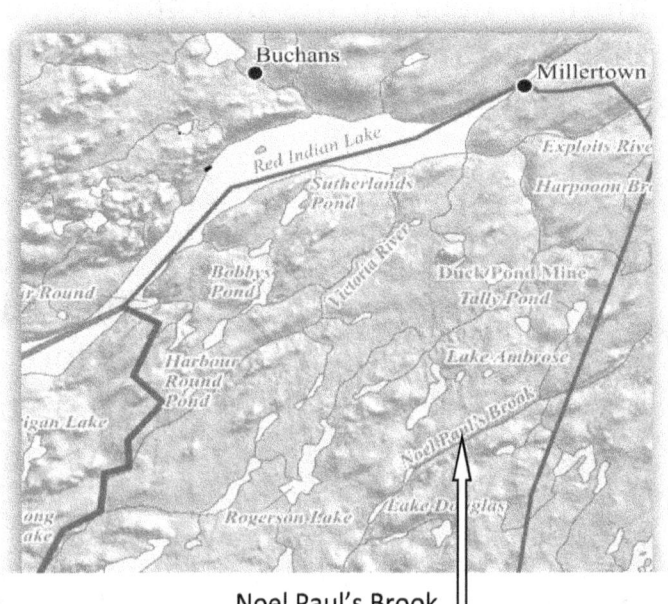

Noel Paul's Brook

Others said they remember him called Noel Boss as well, painting the picture of an authoritarian or domineering character.

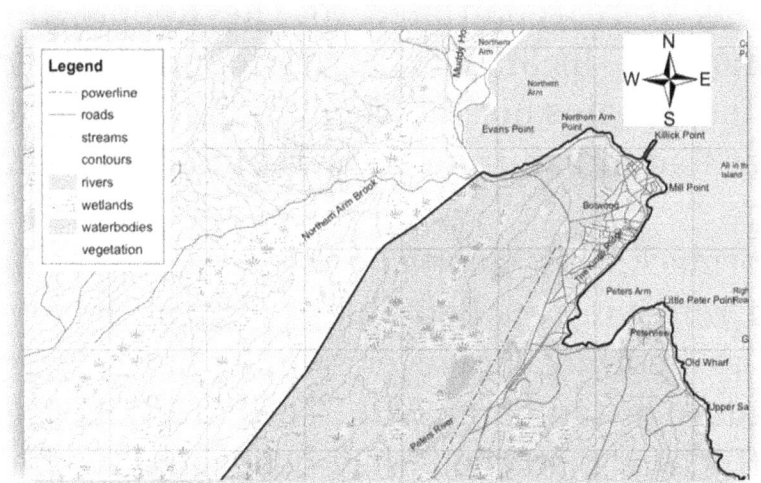

There is plenty of evidence to make one believe that this story is true. Maps show that there is indeed a stream named Noel Paul's Brook and a trap line named Noël Paul's Line in that same area. On the map, you will also find Evan's Point, located near Bishop's Falls, on the turn-off to Botwood. These points of interest were named by Richard Evans, an oceanographer, after his sea expedition in February, 1960, in that same area. Evans was the one who relayed the oral account above. However, negative events such as this one appear to be the exception, not the norm.

This, as well as the influx of more and more fishers to the area, was a huge threat to the Beothuk, who (1) were trying to avoid contact and (2) were being denied access to an important food source. W. E. Cormack was mentored by Professor Robert Jameson (1774 – 1854), a Scottish Naturalist, mineralogist and instructor of Life Sciences, including the study of human beings. Jameson taught at an Institute of higher learning, to pupils such as Cormack and Charles Darwin. After Cormack set out on his trek across Newfoundland, in **1822**, he had no success coming into contact with the Beothuk. Six years after his expedition, with the backing of community support, Cormack founded the Beothuk Institute at Twillingate, Newfoundland. He started the foundation with just a small collection of artifacts. The date was October 2, 1828.

Ignorance, on the part of Cormack and others, lead to the removal of the skulls of Demasduit (1796 – 1820) and her husband,

JE SUIS JACKATAR – SEQUEL TO BACK OF THE POND

Nonosbawsuit. They were sent to his confidante, Professor Robert Jameson, to be placed in the Museum of Edinburgh, Scotland. As of March, 2020, their remains were repatriated to The Rooms, the province's archive and museum in St. John's, Newfoundland and Labrador. But why were the remains not returned to their gravesite in the Exploits region, near Red Indian Lake, to be reunited with the relics of their baby boy?

In the eyes of Cormack, his Scottish Science Instructor (Jameson) and the British, removing the Beothuk skulls was done in the name of science. The Beothuk, however, would never have allowed their burial grounds to be tampered with. The burial site was a sacred place to them. If it was disturbed, they believed, it would lose its sacredness, causing the good spirits to be driven out. Tampering with a grave was a sign of desecration and disrespect to the body and to all peoples of that culture. I wonder if Cormack new of that practice among the Aboriginals!

Cormack acquired records, first hand, from Shanawdithit (1801 – 1829). Combined with artifacts from his Institute and data collected through research at the museum of Edinburgh, Scotland, he is thought to have most of what remains of that once vibrant culture.

The Spirit of the Beothuk
Sculpture of Shanawdithit
By Gerald Squires

There are conflicting stories as to how the Beothuk were treated by some of the British on the Island. The lives of the Beothuk were already in jeopardy with what they saw as pillaging of their food supply. There was also the threat of diseases such as smallpox, measles, tuberculosis etc., which they knew were carried by the white man. Under such circumstances, it was a matter of life and death for them to avoid the newcomers to the island. It is so ironic that so many white men considered the Indian as 'contaminated', yet they are the ones who brought disease to the Beothuk.

John Peyton (1749 – 1829) was born in England, but came to Newfoundland in his younger years, spending most of his time in Twillingate, where W. E. Cormack set up his Beothuk Institute. Peyton was a fisherman and a trapper and the father of John Peyton Junior, who was tried for the murder of the young Beothuk man, Nonosbawsuit, Beothuk leader and husband of Demasduit (Mary March). Once taken from her outdoor environment, Demasduit had no way to protect herself from disease. She died of tuberculosis at the age of 24. Living just ten months after her capture, Demasduit spent her last days in Ship Cove, Botwood, on a Buchan's vessel, the 'Grasshopper.' Her body was placed in a coffin and left on shore for her people to find. History dictates that they took her back and buried her with her husband and near her newborn son, who had also died 3 days after she was kidnapped.

Later, in 1823 the Beothuk woman Shanawdithit, the niece of Demasduit, was also captured by a servant of John Peyton Senior. She was taken to Peyton's residence as a servant for Peyton and his son at Bay of Exploits. When Cormack heard about the young woman living with the settlers, he took Shanawdithit to his Institute, so she could teach him about her people. The young Beothuk woman made a number of drawings and passed on stories about her life, her language, her customs and traditions. She is believed by many, to be the last of her race. She also died young at the age of twenty-eight, on June 6, 1829, of tuberculosis. With the Science of DNA today, people of her culture can be more easily identified. Recently, it was reported, that a Norwegian woman, when checking her genealogy, found Beothuk blood in her ancestry.

JE SUIS JACKATAR – SEQUEL TO BACK OF THE POND

Stephenville Connection To Beothuk

For a clearer read, google 'I interviewed the Great-Granddaughter of a Beothuk by Harry Cuff, 1966.'

JE SUIS JACKATAR – SEQUEL TO BACK OF THE POND

Since the Mi'kmaq didn't write their stories, but handed them down through word of mouth, they are not always believed by sceptical outsiders. We have no reason, though, to disregard the former story, which is backed up by lineage.

Harry Cuff, a history teacher from Beothuk country, Grand Falls, NL, did research on the Beothuk. In doing so he was led to a conversation, in 1966, with Mrs. Anne Gabriel-White from Stephenville, (land of the Jackatars). Anne claimed Beothuk ancestry and Cuff told her story above.

L'Nu or Mi'kmaq

The L'Nu or Mi'kmaq is also a first nation's people, descendants of the Algonquin speaking hunter gatherers. Both L'Nu and Mi'kmaq could be used interchangeably as they both, like their counterparts Mi'kmaw and Micmac or Migmaw, refer to the same Indigenous peoples who were among the original inhabitants of the Atlantic Provinces in Canada, with a significant presence in Newfoundland.

There is controversy over the time period when they first occupied Newfoundland and/or Labrador, but oral tradition holds that it was before any European contact. 'Oral history and archaeological evidence places the Mi'kmaq here for more than 10,000 years.'[2]

---

[2]. https://The Canadian Encyclopedia.ca , *Colonial History, Mi'kmaq*

JE SUIS JACKATAR – SEQUEL TO BACK OF THE POND

The Basque

As early as the 16th century, the Basques pursued the Western Coastline of Newfoundland in their hunt for whale, whale oil and Baleen (whale bone). They frequently took shelter along our coastal waters. With their unique Non-Indo-European Language, they left us with colorful names. One name is Port au Choix, the French Version of the Basques Portuchoa, (which in English translates to Port of Choice). Another, the French place name Baccalieu Island, is also derived from the Basques i.e. Bakailao, (which in English means codfish). The former can attest to the presence of the Basques and it is obvious that Port aux Basques, as well, has earned its name from the Basque whalers. Another good example is that the Port au Port Peninsula was originally named by the Basques as Ophor Portu, meaning Port of Rest. It later morphed into the French pronunciation as Port au Port.

Baleen Whale

In addition to the above, in his book <u>Voyages of Elizabethan Seamen of America,</u> Richard Hakluyt wrote that in 1594 the Bristol Ship, the Grace, found two grounded Basque whalers (ships) just off what is now Nardini's Pond. This pond was named after the Nardini family from Italy who operated a ferry across the Gut River. Hence, this is more documented evidence of the annual visits of the Basques.

As a recognized route, island hopping by various European groups, such as the Norse, Albans, Venetians (Zeno brothers) and the Basque, it is very possible that all of the above, and others, made it to our shores. Our population here on the Southwestern part of the Island ranged from peoples of the First Nations, to Europeans and the British Isles, the Middle East, Asia, Canada (in particular French Acadians from Breton) and finally, to the friendly Americans during World War II.

JE SUIS JACKATAR – SEQUEL TO BACK OF THE POND

The existence of so many diverse cultures on our Southwest Coast proves contrary to the perception, by some Newfoundlanders, that we were a land of a contaminated race. For instance, the Dictionary of Newfoundland English states in the 1852 Journal of Assembly Appendix 110; "In 1841 there were about 250 Protestants. The Roman Catholics in Bay St. George are about half that number. They are a breed of French Canadians (Acadians) and Cape Breton people and called Jack-o-tars. There is a great quantity of eels and lobsters caught here, and in the winter the Jack-o-tars subsist chiefly on the eels. They are lazy, indolent and I am told, addicted to thieving. In the winter and spring they are frequently in very destitute circumstances. They are looked upon by the English and French as a degraded race, thence styled Jack-o-tars or runaways." The above was taken from a report by Captain S. H. Ramsey aboard the H.M.S. Alarm, in August of 1851. Captain Ramsey was on a seasonal excursion to inspect the coastal communities and shipping activities.

Ramsey had many negative things to say about the Jack-o-tars. (Native and French mix). For example, he hoped that the influence of a particular Roman Catholic priest in Sandy Point would improve their morals. This view flies in the face of other newcomers who had nothing but positive things to say about this area, the majority of whom remained. Of Bay St. George, Ramsey continued his negative review by documenting that the agricultural possibilities were not better than other parts of the island. He added that the English were the most respectful of the inhabitants. With such a negative slant to his report, he certainly appeared to be biased in his accounts.

Our own political elite marginalized the settlers of the South West Coast, instead of showing pride in what turned out to be a multicultural population. For example, in the early 1950s, St. Stephen's School held a rich cultural mix of children, including some from the Non-Catholic Newfoundland community, Mi'kmaq, children of the American military, plus the local Acadian Catholic community. It was generally recognized that children of the Harmon, Stephenville area would get a better education by way of the religious order of the

Presentation Sisters. However, the eyes of some beholders saw this mix as a stain on the accepted segregated system of that time. Once again, prejudice raised its ugly head. Someone in the Newfoundland government communicated that such an amalgamation was unacceptable. An article was written in the daily newspaper, the Western Star, that labeled those children as being contaminated. The result was that a newspaper photographer came to the High School and took a picture of a class of students. Presumably this photograph would assure the public that the children did not display any hideous side effects. In fact, they seemed to display qualities within the realm of acceptable human behavior.

Chapter 2

John Cabot – Giovanni Caboto

Three Jacks and a Willie for Cape St. George
The Times

Nearing the end of the Fifteenth Century was a time of great exploration. Christopher Columbus sailed westward from Lisbon, Spain to cross the Atlantic in 1492. A few years later, in 1497, John Cabot (Jack #1), 1450 – 1500, was hired by the Crown to find and to claim new land for England. Under the English Flag he set out on his own journey, with his 1496 patent that was granted to him by King Henry VII. Marco Polo, another Venetian Merchant had previously travelled through Asia. He returned from the Far East with tales of riches and stories of cultures that excited him and his fellow Europeans. As a result, more explorers like Jacques Cartier (Jack #2), were enticed to set out in search of unknown places.

John Cabot
Circa 1450 – 1500

Back then the church was expanding. Western Europe had a very powerful influence on humankind, especially through Christianity. The Catholic Church endorsed abstinence from meat about 3 days out of the week, some 160 days out of the year, or more. The pressure to get fish was paramount.

At this same time, the church was searching for heroes to honor and canonize. Patron saints were believed to be protectors, guardians, symbols of a better way of life. For examples, Saint Augustine was the Patron Saint of 'Brewers', because he left a life of loose living. Saint Christopher is the Patron Saint of 'Travellers', because he was believed to have carried a very heavy child, (the epitome of Jesus,) with the weight of the world's sins on his shoulders, across a river.

The number of saints are numerous, as many as 3000. Religious fervor was a sign of those times and was once a crucial and central part of Christian Life. In particular, Jorge, a Basque and Portuguese derivative of the English name 'George' was the Patron Saint of England and many others, like Moscow, Genoa, Georgia etc. Names like Jacques, (the French for James, George, and John) and Juan, (the Spanish equivalent of the three above,) were historically used, interchangeably, as far back as the 8th Century, maybe earlier, in place of Jorge – our George. Jorge was believed by some, to be a high ranking officer in the Roman Army while others thought him fictitious. He was a legend, a hero who got called upon in prayer, to come to the rescue of many, in times of peril, i.e. in battle, danger etc. Three explorers, Juan de La Cosa, John Cabot and Jacques Cartier, were all instrumental in confirming the theory of William (Willie) Ganong, concerning the place name, Cape St. George, in Newfoundland & Labrador.

There has been a decline in abstinence days over the centuries and a worldwide attitude change towards the church, since Columbus and Cabot's voyages. During their journeys of discovery, they paid allegiance to their Christian God, as is apparent by the names they accorded to the places they found.

Since his landfall on the mainland of North America in 1497, Cabot and his findings has been the centre of numerous scholarly debates by historians and others. Conclusions varied; locations were disputed. Some say his expedition may have been to Southern Labrador; others to the Island of Newfoundland and still others to Cape Breton. Numerous advocates justify their own chosen sites, some with precision, and others with inaccuracy. Much is at stake: historical recognition, a sense of belonging, acknowledgement and potential for tourism.

JE SUIS JACKATAR – SEQUEL TO BACK OF THE POND

John Cabot Landfall

Nineteen ninety-seven marked the 500th Anniversary of John Cabot's Voyage of Discovery to North America. Elaborate celebrations were launched and two replicas of Cabot's ship, the 'Matthew', were built. Members of the Royal Family were invited; Foreign and National VIPs came to Newfoundland. All came to admire and to pay tribute to a 500-year-old achievement. Two governments, the British and the Canadian, recognized Bonavista as being the first landing site of Cabot and his crew of 20. And, even in the wake of Bonavista's claim to fame, St. John's was quick to declare the same honor, benefiting them greatly, from the publicity.

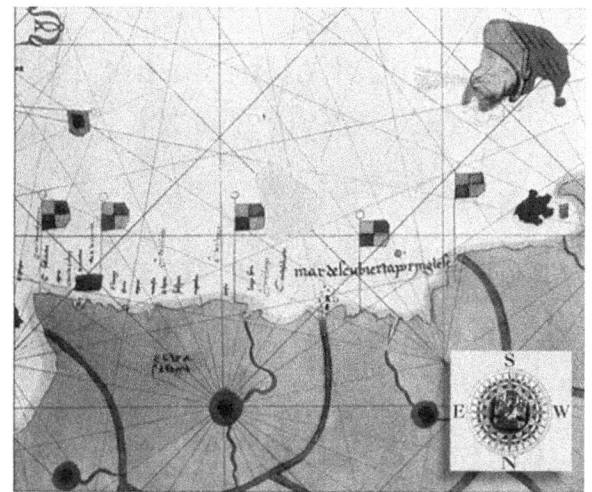

Detail from *Mappa Mundi* by Juan de la Cosa, ca. 1500
(Compass rose modified)

There are a number of documents that prove John Cabot landed, not in St. John's or Bonavista, but in Cape Breton. One of those documents is the John Day letter, which is also available on the Newfoundland and Labrador Heritage Site. That letter confirms the Cape Breton Landfall.

Another document confirming Cabot's route is a Cape Britain Hydrographic Survey of all the coves, inlets and harbours around the coast of Newfoundland, in 1887. This is what was stated in the Newfoundland and Labrador Pilot (Chapter VIII, page 292), about St. John's Harbour. The narrow entrance to St. John's does not appear, when approaching from a distance. In fact, the coast appears hilly, bleak and desolate. We must also take into consideration that in Cabot's time, some 400 years earlier, the entrance was even narrower, with rocks on either side, some of which were later blasted away. A skilled captain, like Cabot, who could navigate large ships would not sail into the narrows and risk his ship and crew under conditions he compared to 'threading the eye of a needle'.

The Newfoundland and Labrador Heritage Site is a good avenue to find information on our province's history. It carries facts on John Cabot's voyages, under the heading 'Exploration and Settlement'. There you will find the 'Cape Breton Landfall Argument' and evidence by William Ganong (Willy) 1844 – 1941, a reputable noted historian and cartographer from New Brunswick, evidence that will fly in the face of all that we were led to believe since our school days.

Proof in the form of a map,[3] by 'Juan de la Cosa' (Jack #3 - Spanish), is the oldest of its kind. It is made on cow hide, and depicts Christopher Columbus's discovery in the New World. On that map there is also a copy of the chart that John Cabot made in his 1497 voyage. When historian, William Ganong, was studying Cabot's chart, he realized and noted that:

(1) **John Cabot, himself, had given 'Cape St. George' its name.**

(2) **The name had survived as a place name on the Port au Port Peninsula for over 500 years.**

(3) **Cape St. George is the oldest authenticated European place name, (not only in Newfoundland) but also in the entire Continent of North America.**

How many Newfoundlanders are aware of those crucial points? Note: In 1534, Jacques Cartier was also highly impressed by the sheer cliffs and unique shape of Cape St. George.

Following Ganong's reconstruction and schedule of events, it becomes apparent that Cabot and his crew did not have ample time to explore North of Cape St. George in the West and Cape Race in the East. Using the same evidence as William Ganong, a History Academic at Memorial University of Newfoundland, Professor Leslie G. Harris, in 1967, reached the same conclusion.

---

[3] www.en.wikipedia.org.>wiki>*map* *of Juan de la Cosa*

JE SUIS JACKATAR – SEQUEL TO BACK OF THE POND

The Adventure Begins

After about a month into their epic journey, Cabot and his men were sailing westward, still searching for new land for England. They probably sailed past the Burin and Avalon Peninsula, which would have been nearby, but were often obscured by haze and fog. Their course was near perfectly on the 46th parallel, north of latitude, too far from the South Coast to be able to see it clearly. Rather, 'The Land First Seen' on that 24th of June, 1497, was, more than likely, Cape Breton, Nova Scotia's most Easterly Point, near Mira Bay.

Cabot was known to have landed in only one location on his whole voyage. A letter found in 1956, written by John Day, also confirms Cabot's statement of events. For instance, Cabot had noted, that after they disembarked, the crew found the remnants of a fire, a stick notched on both ends, a trail made by humans, nets with a netting needle for snares and an odd wooden tool. There was also mention of a type of tall tree from which masks of ships could be made. In addition to a country rich in green grass, Cabot wrote of finding manure, similar to that of farm animals. There were also snares that Cabot was anxious to bring back to the King, Henry VII. When found, the snares had been spread out, little doubt, to catch wild game, more proof yet, of habitation.

Seeing such signs of human activity caused Cabot some worry. He reported that being a small crew of 20, he thought it unwise to advance any further. They had ventured about 300 yards, he added to his chart, the approximate shooting range of a crossbow. The crew then retrieved fresh water and firewood; two staples vital to their journey. Cabot took possession of the land for King Henry, but hoisted both English (George Cross) and Venetian (St. Mark) flags. They then returned to their caravel (ship).

If we step back for a moment, we will recall that Ganong's proven theory, concerning Cape St. George, was found on no other than the Newfoundland Heritage Website. This site is a Crown Corporation established in 1984, its purpose to conserve architectural and intangible cultural heritage. Who might have recorded such an important piece of history, yet conveniently forgot to tell the world about it, especially the Newfoundlanders? It's not as if the finding was a piece of trivia, something that an absent-minded intellectual could easily forget. In fact, there is no question that the academics knew that William Ganong's theory was well substantiated, but chose to ignore its relevancy.

Intellectuals have, against all odds and proof, accepted the bizarre theory that Cabot landed in two places, both Bonavista and St. John's. It's already been confirmed from his charts and La Cosa's Map, that Cabot had only made landfall once his whole trip. But we are expected to believe that John, after landing in Bonavista, left the Matthew and, with a few of his b'ys, jaunted over to St. John's (125 kilometers), to claim it as well. Hey, no sense stopping there; maybe Cabot was so impressed by the 'wild' time he had, that he decided to name George Street after him and King George. The lack of respect for this part of the Island is obvious. In treating us as such, you have denied us our heritage and the future that comes with that heritage. Unfortunately, the actions of some reflect on the whole academic community. You are such a walking contradiction.

(1) **Cavo Descubierto** – The Cape that was Discovered

Ganong supports the theory that John Cabot landed in Cape Breton and it appeared to be the only landfall he made. That fact is not being contested here. In spite of that fact though, Cabot did not give Cape Breton its name. Rather he called it **Cavo Descubierto**.

It is very likely that Cabot had not seen Newfoundland on his outward voyage from Bristol, England. On June 24, 1497, the day of Cabot's discovery, there were 15 hours of sunlight, which would have worked well in their favor. The crew could take the time to replenish provisions and then walk away, unhindered, with a new wealth of knowledge from a faraway land.

Settled back into the Matthew, it is very likely that Cabot's crew may have sailed southwest along the seashore, in order to size up their discovery, before advancing further. Such a manoeuvre would have brought them to the Strait of Canso and proof of even more coastline to come. It is conceivable that they changed course again, turning around to the Northeast, to determine the size of the landmass. From that position, the Cape Breton Highlands would still be visible on their left. With an amazing abundance of codfish around them, they were able to lower baskets (weighed down with stones) and replenish their supply of fresh fish. And finally, Cabot could have sailed away, charting his discovery for the world to later see.

(2) **Mar descubierta por iglesé** – The sea discovered by the English.

Eventually, the Matthew ran out of shoreline, but another landmass, some 10 miles away, was beckoning in the distance. When they reached this new destination (today's St. Paul's Island), they must have been ecstatic at the mere size of their find. From there, they could behold the tall tablelands of the South end of the Appalachia Mountains. Some 40 miles away, the Southern Coast of Newfoundland was visible. A new course was set. Crossing the Cabot Strait, the crew realized that the body of water to their left, (today's Gulf of St. Lawrence), was also significant in size. This, he named **Mar descubierta por iglesé.**

(3) **Code S. Jorge** – Cape St. George

The lookout on the Caravel could now see, behind the Port au Port Peninsula, the snow-capped levels of Lewis Hills, the highest elevation on Newfoundland Island. And, like icing on a cake, another precipice came into view, an iconic, booth-shaped, steep rock-formation that loomed over its lowland. This, Cabot charted as Code S. Jorge, (Cape St. George) in honor of George, Patron Saint of England and of his birth place, Genoa.

It was decision time for Cabot. Northward, but still to the distant horizon, he could see a coastline. This new island was also huge in scope. After finding 2 landmasses, a Gulf and a huge fish supply for Europe's market, it was time to head home. Turning southward to cross the opposite shoreline, Matthew may have ventured into the Bay. If he went in far enough, he could see the hills from the Inner Coast, thus confirming to him that it was indeed a Bay and not a Strait.

(4) **Logofori** – A Royal Courtyard.

Again, after crossing the Outer Bay, there exists the most fertile of land in our province, the Codroy Valley. It has the warmest climate on the Island. Looming into sight, there is lush vegetation and mists at the higher elevation of the wooded mountainside in the background. This majestic view must have seemed to them as a Godsend. Cabot compared it to a Royal Courtyard and named it **Logofori**.

The Matthew's arrival at Stephenville July 20, 1997

(5) **Cape de Luzia** – Cape Lucy.

With saint's names in the forefront of his mind, Cabot rounded the Western Headland of today's Cape Ray. Cabot named it **Cape de Luzia**, which he added to his chart.

(6) **Requilia** – A row of walls, like prisons.

At the most distant Southerly Point of the Long Range Mountains, three large hills loom in the distance, near a towering tableland. To Cabot, from his angle, they emerged as a row of prison walls. To truckers exiting the Gulf Ferry in Port aux Basques, two of those hills remind them of a particular icon and country singer. And so, the hills were dubbed the 'Dolly Partons', after her. Those hills, Cabot charted as **Requilia**.

Several days had passed since their retreat on land. With an abundance of fresh food and water, picturesque scenery and a contented crew, Cabot decided to do even more sightseeing. Excited by the prospects, he wanted to examine more closely what this location had to offer, in terms of resources.

The Way Homeward

(7) **Ansori or Anfor** – Goose Bay

At that time of year, late June, Goose Bay, (not to be confused with Goose Bay, Labrador), west of the entrance to Port aux Basques, was the scene of hundreds of seasonal, migrating water fowl. Cabot decided that **Ansori** or **Anfor** (English translation Goose Bay), was a fitting name for that nature reserve.

(8) **Jusquei** – Jousting of the waters

Cabot wrote of roiling waters, high waves on low lying rocks and high winds funneling down valleys of fjords, creating local tempests. Cabot called this **Jusquei**.

(9) **S. Luzia** – Saint Lucy

When Cabot feasted his eyes on the sandbanks of Burgeo, he was immediately startled by the view. Nothing that he had witnessed so far, could compare to its quiet, peaceful serenity, especially during the rising or setting of the sun, with all its influence. For the second time on the journey he was compelled to use Saint Lucy, patron saint of the blind, to mark the phenomenon. Thus, Cabot chose the name **S. Luzia** and put it on his chart.

Explorer John Cabot, on his charts, uses expressions like C. de Lizato (smooth or flat face), Menistre (the land that has a great wall) and Argair (magnificently prepared altar).

(10) **C. de Lizato** – Smooth or flat face.

Out of Devil's Bay, there is a clean flat granite wall that stands over 1300 feet high, called 'Blow Me Down Cliff'. Cabot's charted name of **C. de Lizato** is a suitable description.

(11) **Menistre** – The land that has a great rock wall.

White Bear Bay in Southern Newfoundland stands apart from other fjords, in that it has bare rock walls and wooded walls, a uniqueness that may have earned it the name by Cabot, as **Menistre**.

(12) **Argair** – Magnificently prepared altar

We know that John Cabot has sailed past many breathtaking fjords. Cape La Hune, for example, has towering hills on each side of the fjord's entrance. It reminded Cabot of a magnificently prepared altar and he placed **Argair** on his chart.

(13) **Fonte** – Source of sweet water

Cabot used the word **Fonte** or possibly **Forte** (difficult to read on a map) in his charts. He may have been describing streams of running water over mountains, from which they could replenish their fresh water supply. Or, he may have used the word Forte, which means caution or beware. The latter term was sometimes used by mariners to steer clear of low lying rocks or clunkers.

(14) **Rio Longo** – The long river

There are various spots along the South Coast where mariners can see a great distance inland, where the topography is on higher ground. Some rivers run reasonably straight and valleys would be quite noticeable. One perfect example is the Salmon River that runs into Bay d'Espoir. That occurrence, Cabot charted as **Rio Longo**.

(15) **Illa de La Trenidat** – Trinity Island

The most compelling proof of Cabot's trip along the South Coast of Newfoundland is his labeling of the three Isles, the largest Miquelon, second largest Langlade and the smallest St. Pierre. When the Matthew sailed by the landmass, from the North the Isles appeared as one. However, when sailing between the Islands and the Burin Peninsula, three Islands become apparent. In keeping with the Doctrine of Christianity, Cabot chose the sacred name, **Illa de La**

Trenidat, to chart that impressive geographic. An important point is that up until 1500 A. D., there were indeed three Islands, because Miquelon and Langlade were separate from each other. After Cabot's visit though, numerous shipwrecks occurred, which earned the area the name, 'Gates of Hell'. Eventually, sand filled in around the wrecks and formed the isthmus that joined the two Islands, as they stand today, as Miquelon.

(16) **S. Nicholas** – St. Nicholas

Heading East, away from the Isle of Trinity, 'Point May' has come into view for the great explorer. It is rugged, flat and diverse, unlike most of the landscape that Newfoundland has to offer. As far as the eye can see, there are lines of marshes, peat bog and a large assortment of water fowl. Cabot charts this vista as **S. Nicholas**. Some relics of St. Nicholas are buried in a cathedral near Cabot's home town.

(17) **Cavo de S. Johan** – Cape St. John

Further along Burin's foot and near its heel is Cape Chapeau Rouge with its bigger-than-life funnel-shaped hill, some 748 feet high, close to the entrance of the anchorage in St. Lawrence Harbour. This obviously impressed Cabot enough for him to give it the name **Cavo de S. Johan**. This Cape Chapeau Rouge, 'Red Hat in French' has been named by locals and found on sets of sailing directions from as early as 1579, and with good reason. It is supposed to have gotten its name from its appearance. Viewed from the sea, it sometimes appears like a hat, red in color. But more importantly, it is noteworthy to remember that from this location onward, mariners like Cabot would be in danger of sailing into thick fog, typical of that part of Newfoundland. In order to maintain contact with the land or even keep their bearings, they may have been keeping their ship close to shore.

(18) **Argon** – Remarkable Peak/Summit

On route to Cape St. Mary's, a trip across the head of Placentia Bay took two whole days. But once they reached its shores, the view was a spectacle of multi-colored birds and water fowl, a chorus of tweeting, chirping and hooting, a panorama of wildlife on the cliffs and in the air. Cabot chose **Argon,** to mark the spot; it was a perfect choice.

(19) **Fastanatra** – Land that shoots rapidly upward

It has been nearly a month since 'The Cape that was Discovered', where Cabot and his crew went ashore. The Matthew crosses St. Mary's Bay, sails past 'Cape Pine' in Trepassey Bay and arrives at Mistaken Point. From here there is nothing but sheer coastal cliffs for up to ten miles or so. Today, a World Heritage Site, Cabot charted it **Fastanatra**, land that shoots rapidly upward.

(20) **Cavo de Ynglaterra** – The Cape of England

Cabot has travelled about 300 miles further East than 'The Cape that was discovered', their only respite. He is learning just how significant Newfoundland is. He decides to travel Northerly along the Coast and finds that it doesn't extend further East. He dubs the location as **Cavo de Ynglaterra**, today's Cape Race, a fitting end to his expedition along the English Coast.

(21) **S. Grigor** – St. Gregory

As the Matthew travels off the Avalon's North-South Shoreline, North America's furthest East Landmark comes into view, today's Cape Spear. It was the largest of the new land that Cabot and his crew left behind, as they set sail for Europe. Cabot named it **S. Grigor,** after St. Gregory the Great. Gregory was one of the Nicaea Council who, in 325 A. D., helped to define the Doctrine of the Trinity.

On August 6, 1497, Cabot and his crew arrived safely in England, after a 15 day return trip. They had experienced favorable winds and an unknown Gulf Stream. They had been gone approximately 3 months.

Dragon Slayer to the Rescue

Red Island got its name from Captain James Cook. Cook would not have been aware of the previous naming of the Island, St. Jorge's, by Basque fishermen. As early as the 16th Century (1500 – 1599), the Basques visited Newfoundland and Labrador, in search of whales. On one such trip, in April month, they were thought to have gotten caught in a storm, somewhere between a small island and the mainland. Being their refuge in an almost certain demise, these fishermen found shelter in the lea of the Island and named it St. Jorge's. St. Jorge's is the Spanish and Portuguese version of the English name 'George'. They named the Island in honor of, St. George's Day, April 23, the day they were believed to have been saved from the elements.

According to legend, Jorge was born around 280 C.E. (C.E. is an abbreviation for Common Era or Christian Era). He was a Roman of Greek origin and a devoted Christian, best known for slaying a dragon. Superstitious, the pagan town, Selene, in Ancient Greece, believed that their only well, their life source, was guarded by a ferocious dragon. They thought that the only way to access water from the well was to sacrifice one of their people each day. Lots were drawn to determine who would be offered up. Only after the chosen one was slain, would the people of the town fetch water from the well. On the day that Jorge arrived in the town of Selene, a princess had been chosen as a sacrifice. Jorge killed the dragon, saved the princess and gave the town back its water supply. The townspeople were so grateful for this gift that they converted to Christianity.

Jorge was later sentenced to death because he refused to recant his Christian faith. He became one of the most venerated saints and martyrs in Christianity and was especially respected by the crusaders. St. George's Day is a provincial holiday in Newfoundland and Labrador and is usually observed on the Monday closest to April 23rd. The English feast day would have been put into effect when we were still under British rule, before our Confederation into Canada, in 1949.

The above Legend, the early naming of today's Red Island, takes on new meaning when it's compared to Juan de la Cosas map. It lends truth to the possibility that the name St. George (Jorge) was being temporarily used, just adjacent to Cape St. George and at that same time in history. It also gives credence to the theory that the name could have originated from the Basque, Spanish or Portuguese.

NOTE: Leslie Harris, Memorial University of Newfoundland and Labrador, concurred with William Francis Ganong on his theory of the Cape Breton landfall and subsequent coasting along Newfoundland's Southwest and South Coast.

JE SUIS JACKATAR – SEQUEL TO BACK OF THE POND

The following diagram, sketched by Bill Pilgrim of Stephenville, is drawn from evidence that is put forth by Juan de la Cosa, in his map of North America. As was said previous, La Cosa has attached a copy of a chart created by John Cabot, of Cabot's 1497 voyage.

In the Cape Breton Landfall Argument, also mentioned earlier, a noted Cartographer, William Ganong, was just one reputable historian who studied and documented John Cabot's discoveries in the New World. Bill's diagram illustrates and supports Ganong's theory, a small part of which is:

(1) Cabot and his crew made only one landfall, that of Cape Breton.
(2) Cabot gave Cape St. George its name.
(3) Cabot spent a month exploring along the South Coast of Newfoundland, before heading home to Bristol, England.

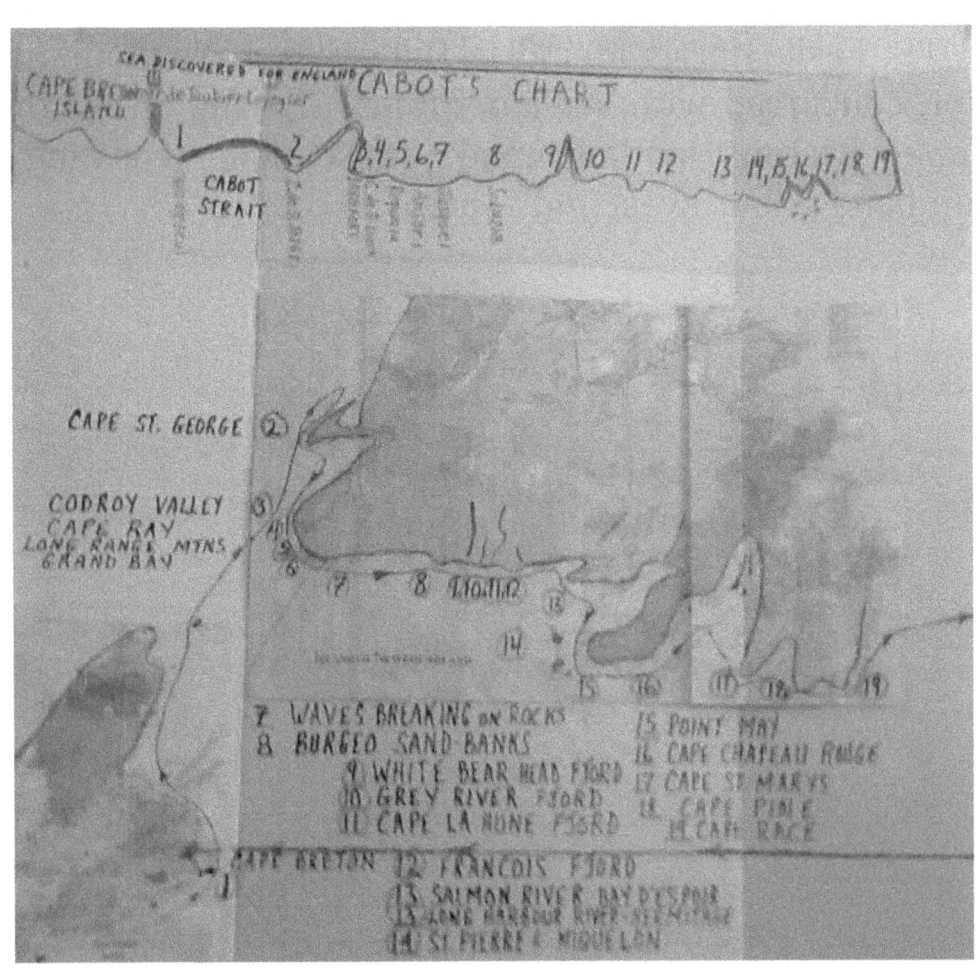

Chapter 3

Location, Location, Location

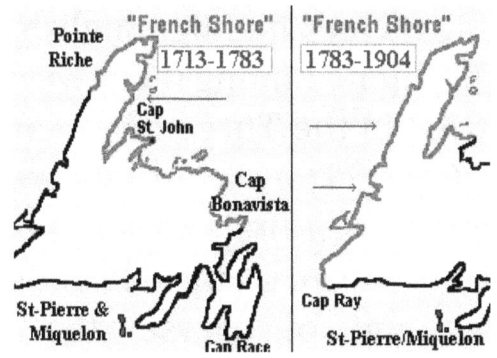

The Mi'kmaq from Nova Scotia started showing up in communities like Seal Rocks, Barachois Brook and Mattis or Métis Point, before the European settlers. They traditionally travelled by canoe, via St. Paul Island, Nova Scotia to Cape Ray and St. George's Bay and migrated all around.

It is widely accepted by many that this indigenous group, although continuing contact with Nova Scotia, had settled permanently in Newfoundland by the early 19th Century. Other historians believe that it was sometime earlier, around the middle of the 18th Century[4]. Keep in mind, though, that twenty Mi'kmaq families came to Bay St. George from Cape Breton. They did so with the blessing of the governments of Newfoundland and Nova Scotia and settled in Seal Rocks in the early 18th Century. In light of this information, I will have to concede to the latter. These Indigenous travelled seasonally to and from St. George's Bay and Red Indian Lake. Here, they remained on familial terms with the French Acadian population.

The French Shore Treaty was also in effect at that time. Her boundary line ran from Pointe Riche to Cap Bonavista. The Treaty of Versailles, though, of 1783, changed the boundary lines to include our Southwest Coast, as well as, from Cap St. John to Cap Ray. In It wasn't until 1904 and the Entente Cordiale (Cordial Agreement), that the French relinquished that right to fish within those borders. As part of the agreement between France and Britain, although fishing was permitted, the French fishermen were never to settle on the Island

---

[4] Dennis A. Bartel, /Janzen, Olaf Vwe, www3.brandonu.ca., *Introduction, Micmac Migration to Western Newfoundland*

and could only go ashore for jobs associated with their fishery, such as drying fish.

As a result of those new boundaries, Sandy Point also became a part of the French Shore. From the days of its first non-indigenous settlers, around 1780, its population increased, slowly, but gradually. It attracted mainly English, French and a Jersey Island mix of fishermen. Among them were the Channel Islanders, who eventually settled in the Three Rivers area of Bay St. George i.e. Robinsons and McKay's. They were followed shortly after by Captain Cook, Navy Explorer. At first, visiting seasonally at Sandy Point, the English, the Basque, more Channel Islanders, the Scots and others from the British Isles and of course, the French, began staying permanently. Numerous nationalities just couldn't resist the pleasant climate, the abundant resources and the superb location. By 1855, Sandy Point had a population of approximately 800, although it was nearly impossible to confirm its numbers.

Sandy Point

There was a constant coming and going of fishers around that hub. Seasonal workers came and went from their winter houses in Cape Breton and/or their land bases in Bay St. George. Sandy Point bustled with activity along the waterfronts and around the wharves and fishing shacks. In order to feed and clothe their large families, farmers grew bumper crops in the fertile soil and kept livestock.

In its day, Sandy Point was the centre of both the Catholic and Protestant churches for the whole area. It had its own Health Centre, a ferry to and from St Georges, a postal and customs service and a magistrate. With the coming of the railway, though, St. Georges replaced Sandy Point as the hub and continued to do so until the opening of the Limestone Quarry in Aguathuna, around 1911.

Today's elders, nick-named sand scratchers (which was sometimes used as a racial slur) recall swimming on fine sandy beaches as children, making their way through the Isthmus to climb the sand dunes at Black Bank and hanging around landing docks and fishing boats. They helped, at harvest time, making hay for the winter season. Memories of hauling wood over harbour ice and walking or skating to nearby hangouts were unforgettable, as were rides on the ice boats with speeds up to 35 or 40 miles per hour.

The coming of the railway train whistled new beginnings but sadly, it also signalled the inescapable end of a once thriving, vibrant Island and a unique way of life, which had all but disappeared. Its last two residents left Sandy Point in 1973. It had been 20 years since a vicious storm severed the land-link to the mainland. With the steady trickling of liviers away from this historic Landmark, death of this community was inevitable.

French fishing stations were set up around the French Shore. One of those fishing stations was that of Red Island, near the community of Mainland, which can easily be seen from that community. Despite the fact that the French were only allowed to

Mainland, Red Island to the right

fish and not to reside in Newfoundland, some French fishermen did indeed come ashore with the intentions of staying.

JE SUIS JACKATAR – SEQUEL TO BACK OF THE POND

Some came to escape harsh conditions that often existed on those fishing vessels or to avoid dire futures back in France. Still others, refugees-to-be, from the French fishery, jumped ship and went ashore at Mainland or at other inlets. They did so, for any number of personal reasons, possibly lured by the newcomers before them, to seek their fortune in this new found land.

Red Island

Captain James Cook 1728 – 1779

In 1763, as a result of the 'Seven Years War' between France and England, the French agreed to use a designated area of coastal Newfoundland as a fishing base only. The rest of the Island remained under British rule. To avoid conflict between where the boundaries for this fishery truly lay, England designated James Cook, Marine Surveyor, to do an accurate Map of the Island along with its borders. In 1767, Cook completed his survey on the West Coast of Newfoundland, paying particular attention to the Bay St. George area. [Note: Many locals continue to attribute the building of two rock cairns at the top of Steel (Cairn) Mountain to Captain James Cook, regardless of the lack of proof.]

Cook was noted for being especially detailed in his mapping of this Island. He would have known that Sandy Point had a sheltered, deep harbour, which was natural anchorage for Royal Navy ships, at that time. Cook may have been the bearer of good news to his navy friends in England, who loved to fish. There were plenty of salmon rivers in this area for fly fishing and there was nothing his fellow officers loved more.

JE SUIS JACKATAR – SEQUEL TO BACK OF THE POND

French and Royal Navy

Because of Treaty conditions attached to the French Shore, both the French and the Royal Navy were seasonal visitors to Bay St. George. As restocking their provisions was one of their necessities, they were amazed and delighted to find plenty of root crops, milk and dairy products and fresh fruit from the orchard. By the orchard, they may have been referring to the fields where berries grew wild in abundance, i.e. strawberries, raspberries, blueberries. Or they may have been referring to home-grown gardens, even small greenhouses that many homeowners kept for their families. Also available was an assortment of goods, made from sheep's wool, which the officers could bring back as gifts to their families at home. There were beautiful products, such as caps, gloves, socks and shawls etc., made from wild fur products, like seal skins and fox fur. At first, settlers had all the land they wanted on which to farm. In addition, the location allowed them the perfect opportunity to sell their products to North Sydney and St. John's as well, if they wished.

In some cases, these naval officers were so impressed with the area that they decided to make this place their home. One such Royal Navy Officer and British Sailor was Victor Lindsay Arbulhnot Campbell.[5] He had been born in Brighton, United Kingdom, to parents Hugh Campbell and Lucy Eleanor.

In the First World War, Campbell was 'Commander of the Drake Battalion in Gallipoli and in the Dardanelles'. There he earned the 'Distinguished Service Order' (DSO). His exceptional service led him into the Battle of Jutland and the Zeebrugge Raid on board of HMS Warwick of 1918. In addition, Campbell served in the Dover Patrol and sank a U-boat by ramming it, for which he could add the award of Bar, to his distinguished service record.

---

[5] https://en.wikipedia.org.wik.vic, *Victor Campbell*

JE SUIS JACKATAR – SEQUEL TO BACK OF THE POND

During the winter of 1818 – 1819, Campbell was posted to Murmansk, in North Russia, during the Archangel Campaign. Endorsed by fellow Antarctic Explorer, Ernest Shackleton, he helped instruct British forces in the use of arctic equipment. For this work, he was made an Officer of the Order of the British Empire (OBE). With the Royal Navy, and reached the rank of Captain, in 1935.

As a renowned explorer, in 1910 – 1913, Campbell was a member of Captain Robert Falcon Scott's expedition to reach the South Pole, in Antarctica. [6] Campbell was First Officer on the first of two attempts to accomplish that goal.

Robert Falcon Scott
English Officer & Explorer
Britannica

However, when Scott made his second attempt to reach the Geographic or Terrestrial South Pole, Campbell had his own role to play in carrying out scientific work in another party of explorers, the Northern Party. He himself led a group of five that was successful, although greatly disappointed. After all they had been through, they discovered that they were just five weeks late, to gain the title. Raold Engelbregt Gravning Amundsen, a Norwegian explorer of Polar Regions had reached there first. To make matters even worse, Scott and his crew perished on their return trip, succumbing to the frigid elements, just eleven miles from their destination, home.

Victor Lindsey Arbuthnot
Campbell
1875 - 1956

---

[6] https/www.archives.hub.jisc.ac,uk *British Antarctic Expedition, 1910 - 1913*

JE SUIS JACKATAR – SEQUEL TO BACK OF THE POND

Among his crew of five were:

    (1) Captain Robert Falcon Scott   (1868 - March 29, 1912)
    (2) Edward Adrian Wilson   (1872 – March 29, 1912)
    (3) Henry Robertson Bowers   (1883 – March 29, 1912)
    (4) Edgar Evans   (1876 – March 29, 1912)
    (5) Lawrence Edward Grace Oates (1880 – March 29, 1912)

Heading the Northern Party (previously Eastern Party), Campbell was also dealing with difficulties. Among his crew were:

    (1) Victor Lindsay Arbuthnot Campbell (1875 – 1956)
    (2) Raymond Edward Priestly   (1886 – 1974)
    (3) George Murray Levick   (1876 – 1956)
    (4) Harry Dickason   (1884 – 1943)
    (5) Frank Vernon Browning   (1882 – 1930)
    (6) George Percy Abbott   (1880 – 1923)

Terra Nova Expedition - Wikipedia

Campbell's ship, the Terra Nova, was marooned in ice. They were able to do some geological work and had been expected back in just a few weeks. Instead, with few rations, ice packing-in-tighter day after day, he and his team were forced to winter in Antarctica. Harsh conditions forced them to stop and build a shelter. Campbell was instrumental in building, with the assistance of his crew, an ice-cave and managed to survive on the occasional penguin and seal. If it hadn't been for blubber off the seal, they surely would have died. See 'Uses of Seal', below next paragraph.

Campbell had other claims to fame, in addition to his service in World War I and World War II. They were what prompted him to

The Northern Party at Cape Adare

return to Newfoundland in 1922 and settle here in Bay St. George, after his naval visits ended. Campbell was able to get grants of land, for free, from our then British Crown. (Remember we were under British Rule until 1949). Victor Campbell had prime property across from the Dhoon Lodge in Black Duck Siding. His land was cradled by the Long Range Mountains and bounded by Harry's River, one of Newfoundland's premier Salmon Rivers. In addition, it had an abundance of fertile soil, the likes of which he had never seen before. Campbell was in awe. With the Trans Island Railway completed since 1898 and air travel in its infancy, Campbell saw nothing but blue skies ahead, our yet to be named, **Paradise of the North**, to carry him through his retirement. Of all he had seen on his travels, and of all the places he could choose, Campbell placed Bay St. George first on his list to retire in. He died in Newfoundland, at the age of 81.

Pirates

Wikipedia, among other sites, alludes to Sandy Point being a benefit to pirate vessels, with its hideaway near the main trade routes of the Gulf of St. Lawrence. Because of its many features, Bay St. George proved very advantageous to pirates Marie Lindsey (referred to as the pirate Queen) and her partner Eric Cobham, who chose this Bay to carry out their dastardly deeds. This formidable couple, Eric and his partner (cold-hearted and ruthless Marie), operated as pirates, out of Bay St. George between the 1720s – 1740s. In their callousness, they left no survivors in their wake[7] and they sank all vessels. They adhered to sadism and cruelty, committing crimes that were unconscionable, especially Lindsey, who showed no mercy. In later years the two went to France, where Cobham (1700 – 1760) became a judge and Lindsey developed a case of conscience; her evil deeds came back to haunt her. She was supposed to have gone mad and committed suicide or, some say, been murdered by her husband. Eric, after her death, confessed to a priest and allowed the story of their lives together, to be written. Their children tried to destroy all copies of that book but one may have survived in the Archives Nationales, in Paris, France.

From Nobility to Pirating and Vice Versa

By the mid 1800s, Sandy Point was home to settlers of diverse ethnic backgrounds, many of whom became attracted to our reasonable weather patterns, our rich fishing and our exceptional fertile soil. Sandy Point was the first commercial centre on the entire Southwest Coast. By the 1830s, there was a noticeable increase in

---

[7] Paul Dalby, *Canada's Pirate Queen*, https://canadashistory.ca., January 9, 2016

JE SUIS JACKATAR – SEQUEL TO BACK OF THE POND

Acadian population in Sandy Point or Jack-o-tar Point, as it was called by some. By the 1840s, there were more French speaking Roman Catholics than English speaking Protestants. Just as birds of a feather flock together, so too the Catholics had their homes, school, church and cemetery on the western end of the settlement. This was locally known as 'Upalong.' The Protestants on the eastern lighthouse end of the settlement had their homes, church, school and graveyard situated there. This part of the community was called 'Downalong.' It is interesting to note that Page 1 of one of the Catholic Catechisms, around 1952, opens with the following question "Who is your neighbour?" The answer, ironically, is "every man, woman and child." Yet religious differences were paramount at that time, and the Catholic Church always taught us not to **fraternize** with persons of another faith. It is a little refreshing though, to see the humor step forward, despite the differences among the multicultural population, as they christened their close communities Upalong and Downalong. We need to keep in mind that the members of these so called 'two' communities, did everything together. They worked in harmony all week long; they fished, farmed and cut wood. They partied together with music and dance; they played cards in the evenings and joked side by side. Ironically, probably the only time they parted ways, was when they went to a church function.

It is notable that during this period, a major commercial centre like Sandy Point got along without the services of a Peace Officer (the Newfoundland Government wouldn't provide for such). It was a busy commercial fishing centre, with a seasonal influx of visitors from around the Island and elsewhere. It is a tribute to the industrious and accommodating nature of the local population that crime was almost non-existent.

In about 1850, the main influx of Acadians began, when the rules of the French Shore Treaty of Versailles were legally still in effect. Yet, in many cases, when Acadians and Mi'kmaq settlers came, the French and English looked the other way. There would have been a natural spill-over of family members from Sandy Point. Also, too, some extended family members of those Mi'kmaq who were brought over from Cape Breton in the early 1800s, by government agreement, could naturally have followed their relatives. As bad as it sounds, when the agreement between the two governments was made, the Mi'kmaq Indians were not placed in the same category as the other inhabitants. They were overlooked, even ignored and referred to as 'savages' by many. Governments, in fact, were indifferent to their needs.

When Newfoundland joined Canada in 1949, the Terms of Union conveniently disregarded the Aboriginals of Newfoundland and Labrador. Rather, Joseph R. Smallwood (Premier of Newfoundland 1949 – 1972) made a decision to maintain the Status Quo. Joseph had said, "There are no Indians in Newfoundland."[8] Such a statement, coming from our own Premier, meant that the Mi'kmaq and Innu were not eligible for programs and services that were available to Aboriginals, in the rest of Canada. In the eyes of the Federal and Provincial Government, these people did not even exist.

So, to get back to the issue of settlers to the Southwest Coast, little regard may have been paid to the Mi'kmaq and Acadians as they flowed in from Cape Breton and nearby communities of Acadia. The Mi'kmaq and the Acadians often intermarried, shared religious customs and traditions and to the British, were often seen as one. They were lured by the rich fishing grounds and the fertile soil on the North side of Bay St. George, in what was then called 'Indian Head' (L'Ans Savage). Acadians had good reason to get away from a repressive English rule in Nova Scotia. By the time they were allowed to return there, after the initial expulsion in 1755, other settlers had possessed their properties. Also, too, a potato blight and wheat fly infestation were ravishing crops in Nova Scotia and Cape Breton, crops that they depended on for their livelihood. As time passed, more and more Acadians followed their old neighbors to Bay St. George. Here, they recognized the many possibilities that this new fertile area provided. As their hearts were always into farming, they

---

[8] www.firstnationsdrum, *Registration to Redress Racist Dirty Tricks*. December 26, 2000

felt at home in this new Utopia, their new Acadie. The foundation of the Community of Stephenville was underway, beginning with Back of the Pond, (Stephenville Pond). When the Americans came to our area in 1941, they were very impressed with the location and its many resources, which attracted and lured the many cultures to Bay St. George.

Just prior to Ernest Harmon Air Force Base being opened in Stephenville, Newfoundland **President Franklin D. Roosevelt, 32nd United States President** (Term, 1933 – 1945), **met** with **Prime Minister of the United Kingdom, Sir Winston L. S. Churchill**, (Term I, 1940 – 1945), (Term II, 1951- 1955). They met in **Ship Harbour, Placentia Bay,** in August 1941, for what would ultimately turn out to be the most important **Agreement**[9] of our lives. The Atlantic Charter, code name Riviera, would change the course of World War II and take it out of the hands of Hitler. He was a German Politician, Leader of the Nazi Party and Chancellor of Germany from 1933 – 1945. On April 3, 1945, Hitler took his own life.[10] A week later, all German resistance ceased.

President Roosevelt & Prime Minister Churchill in Conference at sea, August 25, 1941

Under the terms of this agreement, the United States would send fifty destroyers (planes) to England, to support them in war efforts against Hitler. In return, Europe would allow the United States to lease land on British bases, such as Stephenville, Argentia, Gander, etc. This agreement was seen as vital to the defense of England and its allies and proved to be a win-win situation for them and possibly for the entire world.

---

[9]William R. Callahan, *The Banting Enigma, The Assassination of Sir Frederick Banting*, Flanker Press, 2005
[10]William R. Callahan, *The Banting Enigma, XVIII of Prologue*, Flanker Press, 2005

Now, the United States had newly gained access to air and naval bases in British colonies. With the Lend Lease Agreement, it could provide much needed supplies and assistance to the United Kingdom. They could deliver North American manufactured planes to the Royal Air Force 'by air' through Gander. Because of its close proximity to Europe and its access to North America, Canada's tenth province, Newfoundland and Labrador, was a tempting target for the Nazis. Thankfully, the Americans reached us first. With their military installations on our Island, the British were able to gain lost control in their war efforts against Germany, via air. Up to this time, their ships had been vulnerable targets for German submarines.

In the 1800s, there were a number of reasons why the Acadians from Nova Scotia found South-Western Newfoundland to be a better prospect in which to settle. In Cape Breton, for instance, the population was growing rapidly, leaving less farmland available for children of those large families. To add to their discontent, Nova Scotia also began levying taxes on the lands.

Here, on the frontier of the West Coast, there was plenty of land and no taxes to pay. All the Acadians had to do was to clear and to cultivate, which came second nature to these hearty and hard-working pioneers. So, it was with good reason, that the Acadians left beautiful coastal villages like Margaree and Chéticamp and ventured outward. As fishermen from these two communities, a small number of fishers used to travel by boat over to Anticosti Island, also inhabited by French, where codfish and herring were plentiful. At the same time, probably unknown to them, the fishery was increasing in importance at Sandy Point and it soon became a thriving fishing and business centre for the whole area. The Acadians realized that the community of Sandy Point was even closer to their homes in Nova Scotia and it became their preferred fishing station. With frequent visits to Bay St. George, it became obvious to the Acadians that it would be more economical to stay.

Another prospect, equally as inviting to these Acadian visitors, was the enormous bounty of fish in these Newfoundland waters. Since the newcomers were already proficient in the fishery, apparent from their many visits to the Island of Anticosti, Sandy Point became a vital stepping stone on their quest to the Island of Newfoundland. Sandy Point proved even more welcoming, for there were French speaking fish buyers from the Channel Islands established there. Because this hub was closer to Nova Scotia, these Acadians found themselves relocating their fishing wares and setting up in Sandy Point instead. After some time in Sandy Point, two families, a Hunt and a Pinel (Pennell) family decided to make yet another move. (Note: Pennell/Penney previously believed to be Pinel). This time, in 1843, they sojourned to the North Side of the Bay, approximately one mile east of Indian Creek. There, they set up their homes in the area of Blanche Brook. Eventually though, the Pinel family was known to have returned to Sandy Point, and the Hunt family was believed to have remained in the area most of the time.

JE SUIS JACKATAR – SEQUEL TO BACK OF THE POND

William Hunt was from England and possibly his wife was as well. They were the first <u>European</u> family to "settle" in the area. George Hunt, their third child, was born in Indian Creek in June 1846. **'George Hunt was** also **the first European settler child born in what is now called Stephenville.'** William Senior died in 1885, at the age of seventy-seven and his wife, Susannah, died in 1898, at the age of ninety-three.

The abundance of forests, fertile soil and fur bearing animals, brooks and ponds were all major attractions that were not readily available in Sandy Point. Once the Pinels had returned to their previous residence, word spread about the many resources available at the North side of the Bay. It was made known by word of mouth, to French and English alike, that Newfoundland (Bay St. George area, in particular) had an abundance of resources, a bounty worth chancing in those trying and uncertain times.

With the French Shore Treaty in full swing from 1713 – 1904, vessels came from all over. Many came from France, particularly from Brittany and Normandy and fished the allotted coastal areas of Newfoundland. Their main fishing station was **Red Island**, 1 mile or 1.609 kilometers from the community of Mainland. This Island became the catalyst to freedom, for many, from the French fishing fleets. From there, deserters could make it to shore and shelter, out of the range of the patrol boats.

The French were not allowed, by Treaty, to settle on the Island. But in some cases, as early as 1851, the following surnames were documented[11] as having jumped ship. Their presence here, at that time, would have been considered illegal; the penalty for their crime would have been, according to the Sailor's Honor Code, 'if they jumped ship and people died, they could be sentenced to eight years in jail'.[12] I am sure some other punishments that were inflicted, were even graver. Some such deserters, as they were labeled back then, were as follows:

---

[11] www.ngb.chebucto.org.*1921 Grand Bank Census, Bay St. George Districts*
[12] https//www.es.reuters.com>reuters, *Sailors Honor Code for Jumping Ship*

JE SUIS JACKATAR – SEQUEL TO BACK OF THE POND

Blanchard (Massachusetts) – 1902
Briand (St. Pierre) -1895
Cornac (France) – 1876
Costard (France) 1896
Dubé (France) – 1896
Gillis (Cape Breton) – 1861
Kerfont, France) – 1895
Kerrotret (France) – 1899
Lainey (France) -1896
LePrieur (France) -1900
Lagatdu (France) – 1895
Lemoine (France) 1895
Le Boubon (France) – 1892
LeCointre (France) – 1894
    (St. Pierre) -1893
LeRoux (France) – 1895
Martin (Canada) – 1851 (English/French)
McLennon (Cape Breton) – 1852
Ogon (France) – 1890
Oliver (France) – 1892
Revolan (France) – 1890
Rioux (France) – 1892
Roses (France) – 1896
Temple (England) – 1873
White (Germany) – 1903
Young (St. Pierre) – 1903

This is not to suggest that surnames such as Le Roi, Russell, Tallack, Chaisson, Bozac, Simon and others didn't belong in the list above. In fact, there had to be many more among them. In this case, though, I am giving a cross section of French, Acadian and Continental, who carved out a niche for themselves, before the end of the French Shore Agreement, in 1904. The following list consists only of Acadian French. Note that most of the settlers on the Port au Port Peninsula came from the vicinity of France, while a large majority of those who settled in the Bay St. George district, came from Cape Breton and surrounding communities, thus, the two distinct dialects:

Benoit (Cape Breton)
Bourgeois (Cape Breton)
Cormier (Cape Breton)
Doucet (Cape Breton)

Gallant (Cape Breton)

LeBlanc (Cape Breton)

Some French took the chance of coming to our shores, in spite of the dangers, some even deserting their own ships. They settled in places along the shores of the Port au Port Peninsula, such as Mainland, Cape St. George, Black Duck Brook, and Abrahams Cove etc. There would have been few, if any, Acadian French among them. Still, in the years following the expulsion of 1755, there could have been the occasional Acadian, arriving from the West, trying to reconnect with lost French-Acadian relatives and friends. Some Acadian families lived further to the East, in the Bay St. George district, i.e. Stephenville, Flat Bay, Bay St. George, etc.

There were also some settlers of other nationalities living throughout the Southwest Coast before 1904. Some such newcomers were noted on the South Shore of Bay St. George, in the Three Rivers Area, in later years. This area consists of Heatherton, Jeffrey's, Highlands, McKay's, Robinson's and smaller quaint villages such as St. David's, St. Fintan's, Maidstone, Cartyville and Fishell's. There were, for instance, Channel Island French, English and German, with a splash of up to twenty-four mega languages, so unique, as to be labeled the 'Tower of Babel'. They could have arrived aboard any of the multitude of fishing vessels or patrol boats, from the Americas or Europe, for any number of reasons.

Chapter 4

Jackatar

For approximately a century, British dignitaries were planting the seeds of betrayal that led to the exile of Acadia's French pioneers. Beginning in peace time, the British had taken control of Port Royal, St. John and Pentaquet. Even after the British promised, in 1655, to relinquish that control back to France, they reneged on their promise. Seven years later, in 1662, when France demanded the return of Acadia, the British still failed to do so. Five more years passed, and in 1667, by Treaty of Breda, Britain was now legally supposed to restore Acadia back to France. Again, she refused. Instead, the temporary (English) Governor of Nova Scotia replied in a letter…. "In view of the fact that this province is of great importance to his Britannic Majesty, since she borders New England, it will be neither prudent nor honorable to return this colony to France"[13]. In addition, the Ex-Governor, Thomas Temple, wrote to the British King, "The British Government should never return, to the French, this country, which does not belong to her. Furthermore, it will be to Britain's great interest, to drive away all the French people from America and even from Canada, by beginning now in Acadia."

Under the Treaty of Utrecht, 1713, France legally deserted its French inhabitants of Acadia. As treaties or agreements dictate, under their new rulers, the Acadians expected to be allowed to keep both their religion and their language. Ignoring the civil rights of the Acadians, the British began deporting them 'en masse'. The French Government finally protested, along with many influential writers in Europe, but all proved in vain. "The deportation decree was the result of a cruel policy that was carried out ruthlessly. England braved the cries of indignation that rose up against this violence," wrote Wilfred de Fonvielle (1824 – 1914). Fonvielle was editor of hundreds of articles, from science journals to technical works.

---

[13]Dudley J, LeBlanc, The *Acadian Miracle*, (Evangeline Publishing Company, 1966) p.18.

For twenty years or so, the English deceived the Acadians into a false sense of security. Assured their safety by the British, these peaceful farmers believed their persecutors and even stopped guarding their forts and their coast. Little did they realize that their enemy was already in their midst. Coupled with a number of invasions upon the colonists during those years, documents have now surfaced that conspiracy, by many in high office, was creating an atmosphere for brutal force against them. In fact, those innocent, law abiding, keepers of the peace, had done nothing wrong.

Encouraged by the gains of a few of their piratical raids, the English realized from experience that France was acting rather complacent, doing nothing to defend the honor of its own people. In time of need their homeland had looked the other way, indifferent to the threats that were escalating. As a consequence of their inaction the British started stepping up their advances, reaping the benefits of all that the unarmed Acadians had sewn by hard work, sweat and tears.

No matter what misery and suffering the British caused, those once 'honest and happy' settlers were willing to die, rather than take sides in the dispute or invasions. Little did these Christians realize that their ill-treatment was but the tip of the iceberg, compared to what was yet to come? As quoted by Dr. Webster of the University of Chicago "this, (referring to the treatment of the French Acadians), was the darkest page in the History of England; it was her greatest political crime."[14]

War was declared between England and France in 1690. In Nova Scotia, the English were planning and scheming in preparation and were quite capable of administering reprehensible brutality upon a defenceless and harmless Acadian population. Even though they were no threat to anyone, remained neutral in all quarrels, refused to take up arms (even with their mother country, France), guilty only of being Roman Catholic and French subjects, those

---

[14]Dudley J. LeBlanc, *The Acadian Miracle*, (Evangeline Publishing Company, 1966) p.344

reasons alone were enough to seal the fate of those innocent Acadians.

The Mi'kmaq, one of the first two main aboriginal peoples (the other being Maliseet) of Nova Scotia, were on very friendly terms with the Acadians. In 1752, the Mi'kmaw Chief of Shubenacadie and the Governor of Nova Scotia had signed a Treaty giving selective rights to First Nations Aboriginals. In the Peace and Friendship Treaty of 1752, the Mi'kmaq were promised hunting, fishing and trading. The Treaty Agreement, however, was never honored by the Governor. As a result, six months later, the Chief Jean Baptiste Cope denounced and destroyed the document.

The Treaty of 1752 was not the first Treaty that these Aboriginals had signed with a foreign power. The Pope was the most powerful tool of the political authority in medieval and early modern times. Popes had more power than kings because they were seen as God's messengers here on earth. As early as 1610, to reinforce the bond between them, the Mi'kmaq signed a covenant[15] with Pope Paul V. On June 24th of that year, Grand Chief Henri Membertou of the Mi'kmaq First Nations and 20 members of his family were baptized as Catholics. The chief made a pact with the Vatican (the jurisdiction of the Pope) and the 'Holy See' (Headquarters of the Roman Catholic Church), to protect Catholic priests and Roman Catholic French (Acadians) who would bring priests to the Mi'kmaq population.

A two-metre-long wampum[16] belt, coupled with oral history, marks the historical achievement, the Mi'kmaq's first alliance with a foreign power. Wampum belts are made by Aboriginals to represent a gesture of friendship, peace and understanding, between them and

---

[15] Windspeaker Publication, Halifax, Volume 12, Issue 13, 1994
[16] Native author's view / history of the Vatican Wampum Belt
http://tribes.tribe.net/realdealhistory/thread/

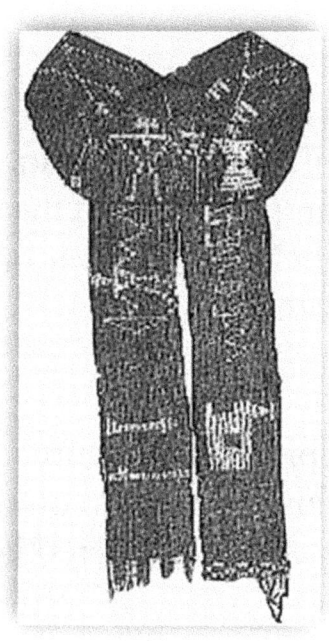 another party, i.e., between the Mi'kmaq and the Holy See. Each belt is unique and uses different color beads, symbols, images etc., to relay a message to its receiver. It can be made to honor specific events and ceremonies like marriage or the birth of a child. In this case, though, the occasion was a covenant with the pope in Rome.

This belt is still held by the Vatican. Mi'kmaq leaders are currently trying to repatriate it, as an important cultural artifact. It reads as such:

The Wampum is read from left to right as follows:

Church Agreement

1. The left side represents the agreement of the Roman Catholic Church with Mi'kmaq Grand Council. The markings on the left represent the seven Mi'kmaq districts. This means that all seven districts joined in the concordat with the Holy Father.

Church built on the rock

2. The second symbol is the church, built upon the rock, St. Peter. The symbol of the church with an open window represents the principle that each Mi'kmaq had the right to accept or reject Catholicism through individual choice. Also, the open church must accommodate the Mi'kmaq

Language and Culture

Mi'kmaq Hieroglyphic Script

3. In the Ancient Mi'kmaq Hieroglyphic script, the council freely grants forever to the Catholic Church the right to build and keep churches on the Mi'kmaq lands, as well as the privilege that its priests may conduct masses and teach in the Mi'kmaq language.

JE SUIS JACKATAR – SEQUEL TO BACK OF THE POND

The Keys of St. Peter
4. The keys of St. Peter represent the grand chief's recognition of the pope's spiritual and political authority in the world, including Mi'kmaq. The keys are placed on the belt to symbolize Vatican protection of the Mi'kmaq nation and its people under the authority of God. No power on earth could attempt to harm Mi'kmaq Catholics.

Black Robe and Mi'kmaq
5. The fifth symbol, the black robe, represents the priest. This figure, together with the Mi'kmaq figure holding the cross, illustrates the union of the church and the Mi'kmaq Grand Council. Each is equal and sacred in the alliance. The small bundle the Mi'kmaq holds, represents the retention of the Mi'kmaq sovereignty and cultural rights within the alliance. Mi'kmaq cultural rights will be especially accommodated within the church.

The Crossed Spears
6. The sixth symbol, the crossed spears, represents the grand chief's promise to plant Christ's lessons of wisdom, truth, and forgiveness in the hearts of all Mi'kmaq, like the spears stuck in the ground.

The Pipe and the Battle Axe
7. The seventh symbol, the peace pipe and the battle axe, reflects the Grand Chief's pledge to follow the path of brotherly love and to protect those who join in the holy alliance.

The Twelve Apostles
8. At the end of the wampum is the symbol for the twelve apostles of Niskam's child, Jesus Christ, who have spread God's message to the world.

Taken from Issues in the Mi'kmaq Community, Mi'kmaw Past and Present: A Resource Guide

Fifty to seventy years after the covenant, the entire Mi'kmaq Nation was converted and firmly based in Catholicism etc. From that time on, relations grew with outsiders, especially the Acadians. When the deportation took hold in 1755, the Mi'kmaq and the Acadians were as one. Under the Deportation Act both were treated the same.

On October 1, each year, the Nova Scotia Government and the Mi'kmaq around Nova Scotia, host a Treaty Day, which takes place on the same date that the original Treaty was signed. They come together, not to commemorate a failed agreement but rather to promote public awareness of the past experiences as they pertained to the culture, traditions and history of all Aboriginals from the province.

The following is just one of multiple incidents of cruelty upon the Acadians at the hands of the British. This incident is relayed to us by Thomas C. Haliburton, in his Historical and Statistical Account of Nova Scotia[17]. 'In this defenceless state, the unfortunate Acadians were visited by piratical vessels, the crews of which set fire to their homes, slaughtered their cattle, hanged some of the inhabitants and deliberately burned a whole family, whom they had barred up in their dwelling-house, to prevent their escape. Soon after the massacre, the man responsible, Sir William Phipps, was rewarded by his Britannic Majesty, the King, for his conduct.'

The following are two extracts[18] that were submitted to the Governor, by the Acadians, in their time of great need, after they were deported to English Colonies. I have deliberately chosen one plea by a LeBlanc, which is my mother's surname, connection unknown.

Quote Number 1: "I, the undersigned, **Francois LeBlanc**, French Acadian, residing in the Parish of Dudley, in the Government of Boston, being a person extremely inconvenienced because of a hand which I am unable to use, incapacitating me to make my humble living, as well as my son, Francois LeBlanc Jr., having fallen sick

---

[17] Dudley J. LeBlanc *The Acadian Miracle*, 1966, p.43
[18] Dudley J. LeBlanc, *The Acadian Miracle*, (Evangeline Publishing Company, 1966) p. 224, 225, 226 & 227

August 20, 1765, being unable to do any work with his hands and having been obliged to call three physicians for treatment, and my poor son above named, having lost his arm and the physicians today, having made me assign for the payment and have taken even my old clothing for payment, and I having nothing with which to pay, I have recourse to you."

I have again deliberately chosen a petition in the surname of my father Benoit, (connection unknown).

Quote Number 2: "**Claude Benoit**, 50 years of age, with his wife and five children, the three oldest were girls: one 20 years of age, the others 18 and 17. After arriving at Cambridge, after the deportation, the authorities of that town seized the daughters and sent them to Mr. Campbell at Oxford. Later, the other children were sent in different sections of the state."

There were reports such as these:

(1) A father and a mother were cruelly beaten because they claimed their salary for fifteen days work. One of them had one of his eyes jerked from his head.

(2) A father and a mother were beaten equally because they complained that one of their children had been dragged forcefully on a vessel.

Hutchison, an Englishman, who wrote <u>The History of Massachusetts</u> said: "It is impossible for me to read at full length all these petitions, the tears prevented me from finishing the task."

We have been led to believe, through Cowboy and Indian movies and through oral history, that the practice of scalping was first introduced by the Aboriginals, heartless 'savages' as they were most often referred to. I would venture to say that the jury is still out on that one. It so happens that the first significant appropriation of this

Native American practice, took place at the hands of American Colonists. These Colonists practiced scalping on a band of encamped Native Americans and took ten scalps. They were a posse of New Hampshire volunteers[19]. The posse received a bounty of one hundred pounds per scalp from the colonial authorities in Boston.

In fact, an order that came to be known as the Scalping Proclamation, in October 1749,[20] six years before the Acadian Deportation, went out to anyone, settler or soldier, who would be paid to kill a Mi'kmaw, adult or child. And, inadvertently, the British would accept a scalp of an Acadian in its place. The truth is that some white folks are fearful of the unknown, of change, of color, of every other race or ethnic group. This misplaced fear often leads them to act erratically. This, of course, is inexcusable. The Statue[21] of Lieutenant General Edward Cornwallis of the British Military has been defaced many times over the years, since the deportation. Being the Governor of Nova Scotia, from 1749 – 1752 and having established Halifax, the statue was erected downtown in 1931, as a celebration of British settlement and as a tourist attraction. Following protests from the Acadian population, the statue was finally removed from the Halifax Park altogether, on January 31, 2018.

In 1754, Charles Lawrence, Lieutenant Governor of Acadia, spewed hatred for the Acadian people. Commander in Chief, he had nothing good to say about the French Acadians. In fact, he made them out to be villains. In spite of his attitude, Lawrence was promoted to Lieutenant Governor, a great honor bestowed upon him in 1754, by the 'Lords of Trade'. This was an administrative body organized in 1675, to create stronger administrative ties between the British Colonial Government and the Crown.[22] The letter to Lawrence read in part, "We hope that this token of our satisfaction with your conduct, will please you." Lawrence was about to prove, in 1755, that

---

[19] https://thecanadianencyclopedia.ca, *Cornwallis Statue*
[20] www.danielpaul.com, *British Genocide, Scalp Proclamations 1749*
[21] https://en.wilipedia.org.>wiki>stat.*citycouncilvote12-4*
[22] https://www.encyclopedia.com, *Lords of Trade and Plantation*

he was the best man to carry out the harshest measures of the deportation of those trusting souls, the French Acadians. There was also another very important figure in England, who wanted the Acadians deported, and that was Halifax, President of the Lords of Trade.[23] In fact, after he arrived in Acadia, he enacted two Scalping Proclamations himself.

There is plenty of proof that individual commanders in charge, did not act alone in the expulsion of the Acadians in 1755. These commanders would and did, have the blessing of the Crown in order to carry out such a monumental task. Between 1755 and 1763, about ten thousand Acadians were deported and, of that number, we know that over half perished, maybe more, even before they landed in ports of English Colonies. Others died because of ill treatment, once they went to shore. The Grand Deportation **displaced** from 10,000 to 18,000 Acadians; the numbers were too difficult to confirm.

In 1763, at the end of the seven years war between the French and the English, the Acadians were free to return to Acadia, but not to settle in Grand Pré or Port Royal and not in large groups. Most ventured although reluctantly, to come out of hiding after that war. Some made friends and remained where they were. Others travelled back to Acadia, in the hopes of finding loved ones and piecing back-together their frayed lives. In the later years of the deportation, some of the Acadians had been sent to France or Britain. Eager to connect with their family members, there were those who made their way back to one of the Atlantic Provinces, some to our Newfoundland shores.

This political crime, 'The Great Upheaval', took place over 250 years ago. Those same Acadians, most of whom also had Mi'kmaq blood (Jackatars), were ancestors of the Acadians and Mi'kmaq who later found their new Acadie 'Back of the Pond' (Stephenville Pond) and vicinity. There are so many definitions for the word Jackatar.

---

[23] Dudley J. LeBlanc, *The Acadian Miracle*, (Evangeline Publishing Company, 1966), p.112

There is the French word Jacques de Terre, which, to some francophone's, translates to 'French farmer.' When pronounced in French, it sounds an awful lot like Jackatar. Consequently, that word would never be received as an insult by some. Other regional dialects, like the Acadian French, would have a different translation.

In their vocabulary, Jackatar[24] may refer to a native of mixed French and Amerindian descent. The more common English term Jactar[25] with its numerous spellings and meanings i.e. Jacktar, Jackotar, Jacatar, Jackatar was originally used to refer to seamen of the Merchant or Royal Navy, particularly during the period of the British Empire. By World War I, the term was used as a nickname for those in the United States Navy. The common name 'Jack', for a sailor, is combined with the word tar that sailors used to waterproof their sails, as well as the seams between planks on wooden ships. Sailors were known as Jack-tars[26] because of the splashes of tar on their clothes. They also applied tar to their thick overcoats to help make it waterproof. When working on board, long hair could get caught in the ship's equipment, so to stop this from happening, sailors would tar their pigtails.

Sailor in Uniform

The big flap,[27] on the back of a sailor's uniform, was originally detachable; it was there to protect the rest of the uniform from the grease and tar that was used in the long hair of the sailors.

---

[24] https://www.dictionary.com>browse
[25] https://www.oxford reference.com
[26] https://en.wikipedia.org>wiki>jackatar
[27] https://www.quora.com>

JE SUIS JACKATAR – SEQUEL TO BACK OF THE POND

The Jackatar Song

The following song was written and composed by Pat Marche and Reg Eddy. The song is just one of ten, in their first recording, called 'Back to Back Childhood Memories'. As relayed by Pat Power from the St. Kyrans, P. B. Power, "Neither Reg nor Pat are strangers to the music scene, in the Port au Port/Bay St. George area. Both are accomplished artists, who have been making music in this area since their early teens. Both artists have played in several popular 'Rock n' Roll' and 'Country and Western' bands over the years and were often featured at local variety shows and other social gatherings."

"The music and lyrics are original. Likewise, while the language is English, the sentiments, emotions, feelings and word pictures portrayed in the lyrics, come from the unique and singularly beautiful French Culture and Heritage of the Port au Port Peninsula. The world depicted in the lyrics is unique to Les Terres Neuviens of Port au Port and Bay St. George. This world was carved out during the 19th Century, by the Acadians and Continental French. They did so on the fertile, but treacherously rugged shores of Port and Port and Bay St. George. In sad reality, this world no longer exists, except in thought and memories."

Reg

"The recording, then, is much more than it's hauntingly, beautiful, melancholic tones; it is, above all, a word-picture museum of the world that was, as fondly and vividly remembered from childhood."

The lyrics of 'The Jackatar', conveys an image, not of a 'contaminated people' or a 'savage,' but of an affectionate, welcoming and easy going character, the French Newfoundlander.

Pat

JE SUIS JACKATAR – SEQUEL TO BACK OF THE POND

The Jackatar

There's a term used loosely that refers to a people
Where roots go way back afar
Some people think there's nothing but trouble
In the company of the black Jackatar.

Some say they are evil and they can't be trusted
No further from truth is this lie
And if you should visit the home of this Mickey
You'll see for yourself how and why.

Chorus:
Their table is for you; they'll share what they have
With care, more-so than you think.
And if you're inclined or hint that you're thirsty
They'll give you their very last drink.

They'll play all their music and you'll sing along
And dance, till your feet are on fire
And when you're long gone, you'll remember with fondness
Your stay, with the black Jackatar.

Some say that a Jackie is a mixture of races
Half Indian, the other half French
But according to Webster, someone made a faux pas
English sailor, is what the word meant.

There's a lesson to learn; from this I have written
Don't believe everything that you hear
Until you lived for yourself, the experience
Stay neutral, till things are made clear.

Chorus:

JE SUIS JACKATAR – SEQUEL TO BACK OF THE POND

For more than a century, Bay St. George has been referred to, as the 'Land of the Jackatars'. The stigma attached to the name still lingers on in some circles and reverts back to the days of our ancestors. Back then, to admit to being a mix of Native Indian and French Acadian was a dangerous practice. For, in the eyes of many white men, you were nothing but a savage and deserving of maltreatment. Communities like St. George's and Flat Bay on the Southwest Coast were largely populated with Mi'kmaq and/or Acadian mix. Yet, even the census of that time showed a significant number, who, in spite of the dangers of ridicule, admitted to being Indian. It is only fitting that those families, regardless of what documents they have or have not, be accepted as Honorary Members of the Qalipu First Nations Mi'kmaq Band. Some others, like purebred Mi'kmaq or a mix of Indian and French Acadian, took their secrets to the grave and, because of horrors bestowed upon their people, probably regretted the day that they were born into that culture.

The use of denial was a common thread for some Aboriginals, to keep their families safe. The same proved true of the French on our Southwest Coast. Parents, like mine, wouldn't teach French in the home, for fear that we would be punished in school, as they were. The Mi'kmaq and the French languages, both Acadian and Continental, were discouraged and forbidden.

It took until 2011 before the Canadian Government officially recognized the presence of the Qalipu First Nations Mi'kmaq Band in the Bay St. George area and, along with it, the claim that those Mi'kmaq/Acadians had landed here, thus **the Land of the Jackatars**. Initially, 24,000 First Nations people were inducted into the Federal Band; and, since then, approximately 80,000 or so from across the country have applied bringing that number to 104,000. It is ironic that, even though the Mi'kmaq first landed on our shores, Stephenville and surrounding communities don't play a vital role in aboriginal affairs.

The community of Crow Gulch, near Corner Brook, is a community of the past. Back in the 1920s it was settled mostly by

Mi'kmaq and the settlement experienced racism, much like the Jackatar's of Bay St. George did, maybe worse. Some from the 45 settler families, who lived there, remember the close-knit and friendly atmosphere of the community. Others can attest to how those Jackatar's (mix of French Acadian and Mi'kmaq) were berated and vilified, because of their race, religion and their appearance.

The area where these aboriginals lived had a three-tiered society, with the upper crust being those who worked the better jobs (i.e., at the mill) and lived in the section of town called Townsight. Those with less pay and middle-class wages lived in Humbermouth and the West Side. The lower crust, who lived near the railroad tracks were poor by money standards and looked down on, by outsiders. Among them were the Benoits, the Youngs, etc., who were previously from the community of Seal Rocks, in St. George's. They were part of the original settler families who had come to Newfoundland from Nova Scotia in the 1700s. In the late 1960s, the community of Crow Gulch was demolished by Government initiative, in the name of 'Urban Renewal'.

JE SUIS JACKATAR – SEQUEL TO BACK OF THE POND

After 248 years, the Queen of England, Elizabeth II, finally acknowledged England's responsibility for the deportation order of 1755. The Proclamation reads as follows:

Royal Proclamation of 2003

From Wikipedia, the free encyclopedia

The deportation order is read to a group of Acadians in 1755

The Royal Proclamation of 2003, formally known as *Proclamation Designating 28 July of Every Year as "A Day of Commemoration of the Great Upheaval", Commencing on 28 July 2005*, is a document issued in the name of Queen Elizabeth II acknowledging the Great Upheaval (or Great Expulsion or Grand Dérangement), Britain's expulsion of French-speaking Acadians from Nova Scotia, beginning in 1755.

Historical background

The proclamation's origin dates back to a 1763 petition submitted to King George III by Acadian exiles in Philadelphia, Pennsylvania. Because the King never responded to the petition, Warren A. Perrin, a Cajun attorney and cultural activist from Erath, Louisiana, in the 1990s resurrected the petition and threatened to sue Elizabeth II (great-great-great-great-granddaughter of George III), as Queen in Right of the United Kingdom, if the British government refused to acknowledge the illegality of the Grand Dérangement.

After 13 years of discussions, Perrin and his supporters in the United States and Canada persuaded the Government of Canada to issue a royal proclamation acknowledging the historical fact of the Great Upheaval and consequent suffering experienced by the Acadian people. The document itself was signed by Adrienne Clarkson, then Governor General of Canada.

Text of the proclamation

Elizabeth the Second, by the Grace of God of the United Kingdom, Canada and her other Realms and Territories Queen, Head of the Commonwealth, Defender of the Faith.

To All To Whom these Presents shall come or whom the same may in any way concern, Greeting:
Morris Rosenberg, Deputy Attorney General of Canada A Proclamation

JE SUIS JACKATAR – SEQUEL TO BACK OF THE POND

Whereas the Acadian people, through the vitality of their community, have made a remarkable contribution to Canadian society for almost 400 years;

Whereas on 28 July 1755, the Crown, in the course of administering the affairs of the British colony of Nova Scotia, made the decision to deport the Acadian people;

Whereas the deportation of the Acadian people, commonly known as the Great Upheaval, continued until 1763 and had tragic consequences, including the deaths of many thousands of Acadians – from disease, in shipwrecks, in their places of refuge and in prison camps in Nova Scotia and England as well as in the British colonies in America;

Whereas We acknowledge these historical facts and the trials and suffering experienced by the Acadian people during the Great Upheaval;

Whereas We hope that the Acadian people can turn the page on this dark chapter of their history;

Whereas Canada is no longer a British colony but a sovereign state, by and under the Constitution of Canada;

Whereas when Canada became a sovereign state, with regard to Canada, the Crown in right of Canada and of the provinces succeeded to the powers and prerogatives of the Crown in right of the United Kingdom;

Whereas We, in Our role as Queen of Canada, exercise the executive power by and under the Constitution of Canada;

Whereas this Our present Proclamation does not, under any circumstances, constitute a recognition of legal or financial responsibility by the Crown in right of Canada and of the provinces and is not, under any circumstances, a recognition of, and does not have any effect upon, any right or obligation of any person or group of persons;

And Whereas, by Order in Council P.C. 2003-1967 of 6 December 2003, the Governor in Council has directed that a proclamation do issue designating 28 July of every year as "A Day of Commemoration of the Great Upheaval", commencing on 28 July 2005;

Now Know You that We, by and with the advice of Our Privy Council for Canada, do by this Our Proclamation, effective on 5 September 2004, designate 28 July of every year as "A Day of Commemoration of the Great Upheaval", commencing on 28 July 2005.

Of All Which Our Loving Subjects and all others whom these Presents may concern are hereby required to take notice and to govern themselves accordingly.

In Testimony Whereof, We have caused this Our Proclamation to be published and the Great Seal of Canada to be hereunto affixed. Witness: Our Right Trusty and Well-beloved Adrienne Clarkson, Chancellor and Principal Companion of Our Order of Canada, Chancellor and

JE SUIS JACKATAR – SEQUEL TO BACK OF THE POND

Commander of Our Order of Military Merit, Chancellor and Commander of Our Order of Merit of the Police Forces, Governor General and Commander-in-Chief of Canada.

At Our Government House, in Our City of Ottawa, this tenth day of December in the year of Our Lord two thousand and three and in the fifty-second year of Our Reign.

By Command,
Jean-Claude Villiard
Deputy Registrar General of Canada

Bias

Danley Woodley Prowse (1834 – 1914), was born in Newfoundand, a descendant of Devon, Southwest England. A noted Historian, he wrote the book, A History of Newfoundland,[28] in 1895. He conveys a deep personal connection to Newfoundland and Labrador and writes a riveting story. I'll leave it to you, the readers, to judge whether Prowse felt any level of entitlement or showed any inherent bias in his writings.

Prowse wrote that, "as colonizers, the French had been failures, always and everywhere." He quotes Herman Charles Merivale's[29], (1806 – 1874) lecture on colonies and colonization as follows: "In only one respect, they were superior to their English rivals. No other Europeans have ever displayed equal talents for conciliating savages and it must be added, for approximating to their usages and modes of life, as the French." "The French in Cape Breton," Prowse wrote, "were just as bad neighbours to Nova Scotia as they had been to Newfoundland. They secretly encouraged the Indians to make raids on the English Settlers and they were always planning the re-conquest of Acadie."

---

[28] Judge D. W. Prowse, *A History of Newfoundland*, 1895, p259
[29] Judge D. W, Prowse, *A History of Newfoundland*, 1895, p198

I believe that the Royal Proclamation above, issued in 2003 in the name of Queen Elizabeth II, is solid proof of the Great Upheaval of 1755 and the suffering endured by the Acadian people, at the hands of the British. This document is powerful enough to debunk any myths or beliefs, made by Prowse or other historians, that the Acadians were not law abiding, righteous people, who refused to fight and refused to give up their religion.

Mercedes Benoit Penney

Chapter 5

Evangeline, A Tale of Acadie

To better understand where our Acadian Ancestors came from and why eventually many were compelled to leave the land that was their livelihood, let's look at the word Acadia, the name of the first French colony in North America in 1604. This colony was settled by French Pioneers from the western coastal areas of France, called Brittany and Normandy. In the first half of the 16th Century, most of the fishing fleets in the New World belonged to France. From those fishing fleet the pioneers came, who eventually occupied the land that became known as Acadia.

Acadia was the English version of the French name Acadie, pronounced (ack-ah-dee), as our Acadian ancestors would have articulated it. The name Acadia was first believed to have originated from the ancient Greek word "Arcadia"[30], meaning a vision of natural bounty and beauty, where everyone lives in harmony. It also refers to a mythical Eden or pastureland, with music and shepherds, so the name was very fitting. If the Mi'kmaq or the French first heard their colony referred to as Arcadia, that name, except for the "r", would have blended well with the Indian place names of, for examples, Shubenacadie and Tracadie. (Both of these place names are located in Nova Scotia and New Brunswick and the word cadie, to the Mi'kmaq meant 'place of abundance'.) It would have made sense that Acadie became the name of choice among the French and Mi'kmaq and Acadia among the English. By 1548, cartographers began to change names on maps and began using Acadie to replace the earlier spellings of Larcadie, Cadie and LaCadie, to describe this Acadian settled area of the Canadian Maritimes.

From the beginnings of Acadia in the early 1600s and through the 1700s, other colonies emerged, some French, some British, which fueled an ongoing conflict between the two countries. The Mi'kmaq

---

[30]en.wikipedia.org>wiki>*arcadia*

and Acadians were known to often intermarry. Those Acadians, who also had Mi'kmaq blood, are one distinct blood line; those Acadians who didn't marry into the Mi'kmaq were of a different blood line. The former is the bloodline to which I belong and into which we, on the south western corner of Newfoundland Island, almost exclusively, belong.

The Acadians, as friends and allies of the Mi'kmaq, were unwilling to take up arms against them or against France. The British were always wary and suspicious of the Acadians, that they might support France in future warfare. The British demanded allegiance to the Crown which also meant, in the eyes of the Acadians, allegiance to the Head of the Protestant Church. The Acadians, as the Mi'kmaq, were completely loyal to their Catholic Faith, to the point of even making pilgrimages in honor of a number of feast days. That faith, coupled with the intermarriage and the common closeness to the land, helped form a strong bond, one that the British could not sever.

Daily, these Acadian people had lived a healthy lifestyle, in both body and soul. They did so as farmers in harmony with their land and with their neighbours. They portrayed the motto that 'cleanliness is next to godliness.' Their large family of ten to twelve children reaching adulthood was a testimony to their healthy upbringing. Their lifestyle helped to contribute to a lower mortality rate than the general population.

Many outside of the French community were somewhat envious of the Acadian's ability to recover salt-dyking marshes into arable soil. The British were also aware that Grand Pré was the area that had the most significant concentration of Acadians, as well as some of the most fertile land throughout the region. To add to the above, the British also perceived the Acadians as a menace to their sovereignty in Nova Scotia, but failed to take any drastic action. Unfortunately, at that time, Charles Lawrence, Lieutenant Governor of Nova Scotia, arrived on the scene. Whereas the previous government saw the Acadians as a continuing nuisance, Lawrence saw them as a great threat. He held a hatred for those law-abiding farmers, and saw their lands as more deserving of English settlers. He further saw himself as the solution to their perceived festering presence and decided to sweep the Acadian influence from the land. Being such a vengeful man, Lawrence was obsessed with commanding his soldiers, seeing that things got done his way and exerted his influence over the area. The previous governors had tolerated the presence of the Acadians, even though they would have wanted them to pledge allegiance.

British Army Officer, John Windslow, Lieutenant Colonel of a provincial regiment, aided Lieutenant Governor Lawrence in his pursuit. Lawrence, along with his subordinate, devised a plan that provided for the expulsion of these Acadians from their land. The concept was to assemble a quantity of ships and disperse those people to the southern English colonies of North America, to England itself and also to France. Although there was somewhat of a plan to keep families intact, with personal possessions, operational difficulties proved otherwise. One of the misfortunes was that sufficient passenger ships could not be found. Vessels that carried livestock, fish and other commodities, were substituted instead. Needless to say, in some cases, the stink must have been unbearable. Another downfall was that, as the vessels set sail for their destinations, (the English Colonies,) local officials would not have been informed or prepared to accept the human cargo.

When ships began to accumulate off shore, near Grand Pré, Nova Scotia, in September 1755, a number of local onlookers became concerned. They were quickly assured, by the army commander, that there was nothing to worry about. Some ships, they were told, were there to bring in replacements to protect the Acadians of Grand Pré over the winter months, others, to pick up British soldiers who had been there for some time. Shortly afterwards, both statements proved to be lies. Within days, the people of that community, and other nearby villages, were under siege and were being expelled from Nova Scotia. A reign of terror began, one that was to continue for years.

JE SUIS JACKATAR – SEQUEL TO BACK OF THE POND

Le Grande Dérangement – The Expulsion

The British quickly began to put their gruesome plan into effect. They built a fence around the church in Grand Pré and called a meeting in the church of all men and boys over the age of ten. By calling this meeting at the church, the first wave of unsuspecting victims were held hostage. It was done in that manner to prevent others from fleeing and to subdue any possibility of reprisal. Lawrence had already given elaborate instructions to his men, that once the expulsion was near at hand, they should feel free to use any lethal force necessary to subdue resistance from the Acadians. He encouraged his soldiers to show no mercy. "An eye for an eye", he said "a tooth for a tooth." All the Acadians and Mi'kmaq could do was pray.

It was three o'clock in the afternoon, September 5, 1755. The scene was this Roman Catholic Church in Grand Pré in the Bay of Fundy. Over four hundred men and boys had been kept hostage overnight by the British Army. They were waiting for a proclamation to arrive from the Nova Scotia government. Nothing could have prepared them for what they were about to hear, the essence of which was: your lands and attachments, cattle and livestock of all sorts, are forfeited to the Crown, along with your other effects. Your money, your household goods and you, are to be removed from this province.

The normal tranquility of the church erupted into cries of rage and disbelief. What evil had they provoked to deserve such damnation? Where were they being sent? What would become of their children, their wives, their mothers, sisters and friends? Few could grasp the enormity of what was happening. Word quickly spread throughout the community.

Some of the first Acadians to be put aboard the ships were a group of young men and boys, the boys as young as ten. In plain view of mothers, grandmothers, lovers, sisters and baby brothers, these young men were marched to the ship, unable to say goodbye to their loved ones. If the young men protested, they were swiftly reminded, by the butt of a rifle, that they were to move along. Having to face an uncertain future away from each other, the elders tried to be strong for the young captives. Being devout Catholics, they took it upon themselves to carry the burden that they were given to bear, praying and weeping to the words of this old French hymn. The hymn allowed them to take solace in the lyrics that bear some resemblance between them and Jesus, during his darkest hours, throughout his crucifixion. This prayer would have likely been their only hope in their hour of need.

> Jésus vit, Jésus vit,
> Nous, comme Jésus, devons essayer
> d'accepter notre sort dans la vie, sans
> se plaindre. Nous devons ignorer
> les biens matériels, comme nos maisons,
> comme il l'a fait. Nous, comme Jésus, devons essayer
> de ne pas perdre la foi, mais
> de porter cette croix d'injustice qui
> nous a été remise par nos procureurs

> Jesus lives, Jesus lives,
> We, like Jesus, must try to
> accept our lot in life, without
> complaint. We must disregard
> material possessions, such as our
> homes, as he did. We, like Jesus, must try not to lose faith, but
> to bear this cross of injustice that
> has been handed to us by our prosecutors.

The sky was dark, with just a flicker of sunlight, as if the sun wanted to close its eyes to the pain and suffering below it. The birds flurried from the tree branches when they heard the cries of the congregation, animals and people alike. Dogs yelped as they were kicked aside by the soldiers, who were in pursuit of their masters, and some dogs fell to the sprinkling of bullets that the soldiers seemed so eager to send. Geese in the nearby field ruffled their wings in harmony, maybe trying to dispel the soldiers from their wicked deeds. They honked and sprayed a shower of white feathers into the air, giving the impression that they soon would take flight to protect their owners. Horses neighed as they stepped back and forth on their legs, showing restlessness that no one had witnessed before. They appeared to be sad, forlorn.

The trees shook as a huge gust of wind blew through the community, picking up the sand off the path to the shore and throwing it into the faces and eyes of the British soldiers. It felt as if all of nature could feel the agony of these Acadians and was sympathizing and saying their last goodbyes. The women and children watched and prayed many on their knees, as sons, husbands and fathers were marched to the shore, protesting in vain. They were kept a distance from their family members as they were boarded onto fishing ships in the worse possible conditions.

There weren't enough ships to prevent overcrowding, a circumstance that only added to their burden of misery. With so many bodies cramped in one place, with no ventilation, it was inevitable that sickness would set in. The air quickly became stale with a disgusting and foul smell that had been left behind from fish, live animals and other such exports, that had been transported by boat over the years. The sickening smell soon combined with the odour of urine, feces and other body wastes, as passengers became ill from bad water, poor food and poor hygiene.

With few exceptions, the forty ships became a breeding ground for disease. Some ships allowed a small group of about eight to ten people to go above for fresh air, one group at a time. But this left little reprieve from those squalid gruesome conditions and the dark gloomy atmosphere that awaited them below deck. The passengers were doomed to this environment for weeks and months to come and with circumstances just worsening day by day. They might not necessarily be the lucky ones, if they lived to reach an English colony. Little did they know what was in store for them when they landed.

JE SUIS JACKATAR – SEQUEL TO BACK OF THE POND

Upon leaving Grand Pré, the ship's captains were given a letter to deliver to the governors of each province as they reached land. The letters gave orders to accept the Acadians and to disperse them so they would no longer be able to unite as a group or a people. This was a time when there was a great deal of prejudice throughout the world. Wars were fought in the name of religion and land disputes. The Great Deportation was no exception. In the English colonies, there was a hatred of Catholics such that, if they reached the colonies alive, they were treated as slaves.

Next day, dawns early light revealed a number of ships assail, anchored just offshore. Onshore, the first movement of the soldiers was then followed by the tempo of increased activity of the settlers. Selected household goods were moved to the beach. Intuitively, being harvesting time, these people still felt obligated to take care of the hay, fill the cellars and feed the livestock. In the confusion one child was heard asking, "Mama, will we need our sabots (clogs)."

As the morning progressed and more and more neighbors made their way to the beach with their wares, a sense of foreboding gradually overwhelmed the group. They became even more apprehensive about their husbands and young sons, fathers and grandfathers. Unable to deal with the physical reality of what was expected of them, they looked for spiritual guidance. They began to sing and pray.

As the day advanced the dories continued to move people from the beach to the cargo vessels. Groups of people lined the beaches, as convoys of dories went back and forth to the waiting ships. This turned into anxiety for some, as they realized that many of their family members weren't among them. With the limited capacity of the rowboats, it took more than one trip or boat to transport the many large families that were destined to go aboard. It quickly dawned on them that their household items, along with many previous heirlooms, would not be put on the ship as promised, as overcrowding was quickly becoming a reality.

Antoinette's treasured fine china and silverware set reflected in the sunlight, where it was left at tide-water. Cornelius was hauling the bunk chain to the beach when he realized that his ox, Nicodemus, couldn't be taken with him; he dropped the chain where he stood. Molly and her mother momentarily paused in the front door of their family home to overlook the scene unfolding before their eyes. At the age of sixteen, Molly's thoughts couldn't help but go back to her last moments with Anselm, as she subconsciously twisted the Spanish coin he had given her, the one that hung around her neck on a piece of twine.

Initially, the British rounded up thousands of liviers from Grand Pré and surrounding districts. By orders of the soldiers, later in the day, animals were being removed from the barns. The soldiers began to set fire to the store-houses, barns, sheds and out-houses. Euzeb forgot his sling shot for the moment and reminded his mother that they still hadn't gotten the turnips from the cellar. Bellowing clouds of black smoke hovered over Grand Pré.

Mileage LeBlanc had broken his leg last year when he fell under his horse-drawn sleigh of wood. Janette Bourgeois had been blinded as a young woman, when she was accidentally splashed in the face with lye. Marie Gabriel was heavily burdened with child. Those were the last family members to be removed from the homes. They were transported by horse-buggy, by coaches and, in one instance, placed upon blankets in a wheelbarrow. These, and other handicapped individuals had to be aided on their long journey to the beach, and manually carried to the carts, boats etc.

Necessities, vital to survival, like spinning wheels, leather working tools, axes, saws and cart wheels were some of the items that began piling up on the beach. There were others, equally as important such as pit saws, plow shaves, scythes, hoes, water buckets, rakes, pick-axes and chamber pots. Winter items like mukluks, mitts, caps, parkas, socks, coils of rope, snowshoes and hand sleds were also strewn about.

Not knowing their destination, the families could only visualize where they would land, what they might need and when. They had to be extremely mesmerized at the lack of information, for all of their belongings were equally important to their survival. Little did they know that five years from now, most of those items would still be lying on the beach, as a testimony to just how complete the expulsion had been. Their destination was determined by logistics, regimentally, rather than the essentials for their survival.

Although Lawrence, no doubt, considered himself a very busy diligent governor, he justified time and men to travel to Grand Pré to choose six of the Acadian's finest horses, a black one for himself, and a white one for his secretary. Even in carrying out commands for the British regime, Lawrence did not have to be as callous as he was. For example, it was not in his mindset to make provisions to keep the families together. If family members were at large, which was common in the chaos, they could be destined then, to another ship, and possibly never seen again by their families. Still, Lawrence gave his men strict orders to sail without them.

It wasn't until fully boarded that the Acadians realized what meager accommodations were available to them. They soon learned that the vessels reeked from the stench of the previous cargo that it had been previously laden with, such as animal furs and salt fish. "Mon Dieu!" said Anne-Marie, "I hope Julianna remembered to take the spinning wheel." And then the curse continued on. They're now being told that the vessel has no room for anyone else. Other members of the family will have to board another vessel.

Ship after ship hoarded up women, children and elderly, making many view these horrific scenes as they burned their villages to the ground. Because a few hundred managed to get away into the woods, the British burned even their crops, in the hopes that they wouldn't be able to survive the winter. As passengers loaded the ships, they carried only what they could use for their immediate comfort, if lucky, a blanket or a pillow. As Sarah gets up from her bench, she is immediately pushed toward the vessels laden with human cargo. She looks back at the homes in flames. She clutches young Ivan close. He cries out "Mais pourquoi, Mima! pourquoi?"

All ships were loaded and ready to depart when a fierce storm prevented the ships from sailing. This was just the first of two storms that would significantly delay the ships from leaving Grand Pré. Some of these vessels were destined for the English Colonies of Eastern North America, while others were heading for England or France. It staggers the imagination that, to add to their torment, the weather even seemed to be conspiring against these peaceful Acadians. Fate was not on their side. Just waiting out these storms would prove to be disheartening for all those cramped souls onboard, a foreboding beginning to what would become a horrific journey.

Injuries were common on these vessels. The almost constant swaying bounced people around, so it would be close to impossible to avoid injury from smashing up against each other, or against the ship itself. Once injuries occurred, there was no way to take care of the wounds and keep cuts from getting infected. Once infection set in, a passenger had little chance of recovering and making it to shore. There is no way to overstate the conditions on board these ships. I cringe at the very thought of men, women and children being subjected to such brutality. It's difficult to believe that Christians could inflict such atrocities on fellow Christians, considering this command, which is based on the words of Jesus in the Sermon on the Mount, "Do unto others as you would have them do unto you."[31] What the Acadians endured, at the hands of the British, was wicked, brutal and barbaric. This was cruel treatment for a community of people, most of whom always tried to avoid confrontation and to lead a peaceful and tranquil lifestyle. As many of the forty ships set sail for the English colonies, one family of Jacqueline Benoist, age 82, believed to be the first Acadian born in Acadia, was among the exiled. Members of her family embarked on different ships, to different destinations such as Maryland, Virginia or Massachusetts. Some of those family members never saw each other again.

---

[31] www.dictionary.com *browse .do.unto Luke 6:31 Bible*

On some of the ill-fated ships the captains had retrieved geese from the farms at Grand Pré. They, with their crew of soldiers, prepared, cooked and ate those geese while the starving passengers looked on. Most of the old, sick and infirm died on the ships, leaving a trail of bodies behind as they were thrown into the sea. On one ship that landed in Philadelphia, the passengers were sick with smallpox. The governor refused to allow the riff-raff, (disreputable or undesirable people), as they were sometimes called, to go ashore. Instead, they were confined to the ship's quarters for three more months, left again in the cold, with no place to sleep, no sanitation and no food, except smoked meat, dry bread and dirty water. The British had allotted one pound of beef, two pounds of bread and five pounds of flour per person for the whole trip. Among the sick there was a young child, a blind middle-aged woman, a number of older men, decrepit and ill and a number of young girls, to name a few. The Acadians had large families, and on average, there were three girls to every household.

Being turned away by the Governor of Philadelphia was another blow to the helpless passengers on board. They had watched so many die on the trip from Grand Pré. Imagine how relieved they would have felt when they reached land and how disheartened they must have felt to be rejected once more; starved and left to the elements over half of them died. The total death count reached about ten thousand. Most died at sea, but many also died after they arrived at an English colony.

One ship, the 'Edward Cornwallis,' for example, lost two hundred and ten of its four hundred and seventeen passengers on the voyage. As passengers died, and were thrown overboard, they were even denied the dignity of a service, like the 'Last Rites.' that were so important to these devout Catholics. Before reaching the colonies, the ship's human cargo would have suffered immensely. They would have suffered from seasickness, starvation or succumbed to a multitude of health problems brought on by disease, such as smallpox or typhus. Being isolated on farms had prevented these farmers from building immunity to some of societies diseases, such as they encountered on their journey. What they would face transcended the boundaries of human decency.

We have no way to calculate the names of those who died at sea, as no names were taken. Ships captains used shipping manifestos to record how many were shipped, as they would with cargo, and how many tons, but no consideration for the fact that they were human beings. The captains would have kept logs on which to calculate their pay, when they delivered their cargo. The fatality rate during those deportation years was 53%. In fact, their treatment would later be classified by some as inhumane, by others as genocide. Some ships didn't even make it to shore, but capsized in unruly or stormy seas. Others made it to shore, only to be treated as paupers and thieves. Drop-off points included colonies in the Caribbean as well as East and West Florida.

There was even a law enacted which allowed the British to take the children away from their parents and use them in a way that allowed them to earn their keep, as slaves for private families, workers on the farms, or hard labor. They had children pulled from their arms, screaming and crying. Many died from grief or epidemics or were sent to concentration camps, or jail, in Britain or France. Of the remaining Acadians, those who reached colonies were not wanted there either. Strangers despised both their nationality and their Catholic religion. Few tragedies can compare to the atrocities suffered at the hands of the British, for the suffering continued for months and years.

Governor Lawrence even proclaimed that every Indian, over the age of sixteen, be made prisoner or killed. This ruling affected the Acadians deeply. As allies and close relations, these two groups were being targeted, the French Acadians and/or the Indigenous group, the Mi'kmaq. In fact, the British, on many occasions, saw the Acadians and the Mi'kmaq as one race, going as far as to offer thirty-five pounds sterling for a Mi'kmaw scalp, but inadvertently accepting Acadian scalps as well.

JE SUIS JACKATAR – SEQUEL TO BACK OF THE POND

It is documented that during these years a small family of Mi'kmaq were shot and scalped when they were seen resting by a river stream. Scalping went on for years and the British could get good money, whether an Indian was brought in, dead or alive. If alive they could be sold for slaves. In the eyes of the onlookers, the Acadians were considered below the black slave and were made to live among the black and work with or below them. In fact, General Cornwallis had admitted, in a document, that he wished to see the Acadian race obliterated. To those who witnessed or collected and studied the oral history through research, these barbaric acts really stood out as ethnic cleansing and an intention to wipe out a race of people.

In a second wave of deportation, some Acadians were sent back to their homeland, France, and others to England, where many were looked upon as enemies of the British and jailed. Some of these same Acadians were eventually able to make their way to Louisiana. Their descendants, the Cajuns, continue to speak French and to farm, just as their ancestors, the Acadians, had taught them. The Acadian expulsion was, at the very least, another stain on the history of Empire building. Some of the Acadians arrived in American colonies and as time passed, they became allies of the Americans. However, they did so very reluctantly, at first. Ironically, once these Americans realized that the riff-raff could be useful as allies, their attitudes changed. The American Colonists, with the assistance of their new allies, the Acadians, were then able to defeat the British in the Revolutionary War of 1776. Note: The return to Acadie was always on the minds of these banished people.

JE SUIS JACKATAR – SEQUEL TO BACK OF THE POND

Evangeline, a Tale of Acadie
Written by William Wadsworth Longfellow
and published in 1847

The following is an excerpt from a twenty-page epic poem. Set during the time of the expulsion of the Acadians, this poem follows an Acadian girl named Evangeline and her search for her long-lost love 'Gabriel'. William Wadsworth Longfellow had never heard of, nor witnessed, such faithfulness and persistence by a lover or spouse, as was told to him by Nathaniel Hawthorne, who claimed that the following story was originally communicated to him by a French Canadian.

After being separated from each other in the Expulsion of 1755, this French Acadian woman had kept wandering from place to place in search of her husband and lover. Years later, when she finally found him, he was on his death bed. As the story went, Gabriel died in her arms and she died shortly after, broken hearted.

Wadsworth's biographer, Charles Calhoun, assures us of Longfellow's intention to reflect the basic human truth of the expulsion of the Acadians. His poem authenticates the belief that the Acadians were good people, undeserving of any negative criticism.

Henry Wadsworth Longfellow was a renowned American poet and educator, famous also for his written works, like Paul Reverés Ride, and Poems of Slavery. Longfellow writes of the Expulsion from Nova Scotia, Grand Pré in particular, of the Acadians, the same group of people that I spoke of earlier. It is not well known that we are related to those Acadians that were deported from the Maritime Provinces in 1755 and onward. But some descendants of those approximately eleven thousand Acadians ended up settling in places such as Sandy Point and later to areas in and around Stephenville. Many of those same people were a mixture of Mi'kmaq/French, and from there we had the evolution of Newfoundland's first bilingual society. This class of people, however, was unfortunately misunderstood by some of our fellow Newfoundlanders, especially the 'merchant political establishment.' Failing to recognize this linguistic phenomenon and bogged down as usual in their cocoon of entitlement, the establishment called these Acadian newcomers 'Jack-o-tars'.

The word 'epic', which Longfellow uses to describe his style of poem, in itself, means heroic. Although he wrote from an independent perspective about the Acadian people, Longfellow was moved by the beauty and strength of the women's devotion and by the dedication, patience and endurance of the men and women as they lived the traditional way of life. Longfellow noted in the poem that they worked hard on their farms and that life had been pleasant in Grand Pré. He noted that they had affection and love for each other and great hopes and dreams for the future. The poet even referred to Grand Pré as the "home of the happy." Nowhere, as he researched the lives of those Acadians, did he discover examples of animosity or hatred. On the contrary, he learned that the deportation of its people took place after these farmers remained neutral in the ongoing conflicts between the English and the French.

From the forest, the farms and the pasture land, the Acadian community was self-sustaining in food, shelter and clothing, not to mention that their entertainment abilities were legendary. They had great devotion to their faith and to their way of life. They looked upon a rainy day with just as much enthusiasm as they did a sunny day, for they realized that each contributed to a good crop. Undoubtedly, we could say, without hesitation, that they were one with the earth. And in the face of adversity, they used humor in big doses to help carry them through. What became obvious to this American, Longfellow, was that the Acadian people were industrious and righteous. What he saw, he beautifully portrayed in his poem 'Evangeline.'

Below is an excerpt of the most endearing insights into the community of Acadians, <u>Evangeline, A Tale of Acadie</u> by Henry Wadsworth Longfellow.

JE SUIS JACKATAR – SEQUEL TO BACK OF THE POND

Evangeline, A Tale of Acadie

This is the forest primeval. The murmuring pines and the hemlocks,
Bearded with moss, and in garments green, indistinct in the twilight,
Stand like Druids of eld, with voices sad and prophetic,
Stand like harpers hoar, with beards that rest on their bosoms.
Loud from its rocky caverns, the deep-voiced neighboring ocean
Speaks, and in accents disconsolate answers the wail of the forest.

This is the forest primeval; but where are the hearts that beneath it
Leaped like the roe, when he hears in the woodland the voice of the huntsman
Where is the thatch-roofed village, the home of Acadian farmers?
Men whose lives glided on like rivers that water the woodlands,
Darkened by shadows of earth, but reflecting an image of heaven?
Waste are those pleasant farms, and the farmers forever departed!
Scattered like dust and leaves, when the mighty blasts of October
Seize them, and whirl them aloft, and sprinkle them far o'er the ocean
Naught but tradition remains of the beautiful village of Grand-Pré.

Ye who believe in affection that hopes, and endures, and is patient,
Ye who believe in the beauty and strength of woman's devotion,
List to the mournful tradition, still sung by the pines of the forest;
List to a Tale of Love in Acadie, home of the happy.

When the Acadians started showing up in Newfoundland, they were greeted with little enthusiasm by the governing English establishment, but the Indigenous welcomed them.

Chapter 6

First Families of New-found-Acadie

Before it got its name, Stephenville consisted of three main areas:

(1) The Parish – on West Street, St. Stephen's Church, Graveyard, Priest's House, Convent and St. Stephen's Primary, Elementary and High Schools.

(2) The Village, pronounced by the French Acadians who lived there, as if it were our own Newfie dialect for look, (le), followed by ville, followed by ashhh, until it rolled off their tongue as LeVillage, was the area from the Parish, down through Main Street and ended up at Blanche Brook.

(3) The area east of Blanche Brook near the shoreline, including Stephenville Pond, (now Port Harmon) to the Indian Head Mountain Range, known sometimes as Indian Creek, Indian River or more so, as Indian Head or Back of the Pond.

James/Jimmy Gallant, (b. June 14, 1944), was kind enough to share the following letter written by Agnes Gallant. In it she confirms that Stephen Gallant was taken from L'Anse aux Savage, (now Stephenville) to Margaree, Nova Scotia, to be baptised. The year she gives in her letter, of that trip to Margaree, however, contradicts the year that I have, 1848.

Agnes Gallant was a direct descendant of Stephenville's original settler family. In addition to confirmation about that her family history, she also portrays a unique perspective on a number of issues, such as the fishery, the parish and the clergy.

JE SUIS JACKATAR – SEQUEL TO BACK OF THE POND

Letter by Agnes Gallant

In the year 1845, Étienne LeBlanc and his wife Ann Marie Cormier sailed by schooner from Margaree, Cape Breton, Nova Scotia to Newfoundland. They settled in Indian Cove; another name used by the French to identify Stephenville. Also accompanying him on the trip, were his daughter Theotiste and her husband Felix Gallant. Their first child, Stephen, was born in 1845. The child was brought to Margaree for christening in 1846. Having experienced a very mild winter 1845/1846, they encouraged other family members to come to Newfoundland. All but two, of Étienne LeBlanc's sons came. The LeBlanc's, who are now residing in Margaree Forks and vicinity, are their descendants.

Stephen had been taken to Margaree or Chéticamp for Baptism, because there was no regular visitation by priests on the West Coast of Newfoundland. Research done by Reverend Michael Brosnan found evidence of the fact, that only one priest visited that coast prior to 1848, that is, other than the occasional visits made by chaplains. (Note: A priest is an ordained member of the Roman Catholic religion, while a chaplain is traditionally non-ordained). Chaplains came, from time to time, on Canadian Government lighthouse boats or with French fishing fleets. Brosnan reported that Reverend William Hearn had trekked across the Island, accompanied by an Indian Guide. The two left St. John's in about 1820. Therefore, in all probability, this journey preceded that of Cormack, who is believed to have been the first white man to walk across Newfoundland, from sea to sea. Cormack's journey is dated as 1822.

The question arises, as to why a condition of spiritual destitution existed for such a long period. It was probably because of the need of a priest with great physical endurance and with ability to communicate in both French and English languages. There also existed a disturbed political situation, because of French treaties. Because of these existing treaties, the French claimed exclusive rights to fisheries along the coast, from Cape St. John to Cape Ray.

Furthermore, France objected to colonization. Meanwhile, the English, in theory, rejected these exclusive rights of the French and claimed that English subjects had concurrent rights to those fisheries, provided they did not 'interrupt' the French. England also claimed the right to settle in the area provided they did not interrupt the French fishing operations. But, in practice, England acknowledged the French claims by discouraging all settlement, thus making grants of land impossible to obtain. In spite of the above, settlements along the West Coast were still happening. Many settlers did some fishing, but some were interested primarily in farming, particularly settlers from Cape Breton.

In 1848, Most Reverend John T. Mullock, along with Reverend R. Condon, visited Sandy Point and even visited as far north as Ferrole on August 27, 1848. By 1850, Father Alexis Belanger arrived on the West Coast. He had been born January 18, 1808, at Saint Roch-des Aulnaies in County L'Islet, Quebec, a town on the North Shore of the St. Lawrence River, approximately fifty miles from Quebec City. Belanger was ordained in 1835, worked in the province of Quebec and, in 1839 he went to the Magdalen Islands. Leaving there, he spent the winter of 1848-1849 in Paraquet and Rustico, followed by a missionary visit to Labrador. From Labrador, Belanger joined a schooner at Blanc Sablon for Sandy Point, arriving in Bay St. George September 7, 1850.

By 1852, Belanger had built a house and when Bishop Mullock and Reverend John Vereker visited, this building was in existence. A church was under construction by April, 1855, four months after Pope Pius IX defined the Dogma of the Immaculate Conception. The church was blessed and dedicated to the Mother of God, 'The Church of the Immaculate Conception.' It later became the Pro-Cathedral, temporarily serving as a cathedral in the diocese, to which the Bishop was associated.

Father Belanger also made visits to Codroy Valley, Highlands, various parts of the Port au Port Peninsula, Bay of Islands and Cow Head. He completed a church and a small dwelling on the North Shore of Grand River. After eighteen years of service, he died on the anniversary of his arrival in Sandy Point, September 7, 1868. His saddened congregation had his body embalmed (preserved with spices) and brought to his birth place, by schooner, where he was buried September 29, 1868. Frederick Halbot, Hector McDonald and John Cashin, accompanied his remains. Their signatures are present in the death register, alongside signatures of the many priests who attended the burial.

Bishop Mullock then recruited the service of Reverend Thomas Sears, native of Ventry, near the town of Dingley, County Kerry, Ireland. He arrived at the Gravels (Port au Port West) through the kindness of a Captain Jackman, who was going to Bay of Islands for a cargo of fish. Father Sears came from Port Mulgrave, Strait of Canso, to Newfoundland, at Bishop Mullock's request. He travelled the remaining thirty miles, from the Gravels to Sandy Point, on foot.

There was no mail service, no schools, no civil authority and no roads – "just a howling wilderness", as stated by Father Sears. On arrival, Sears started a building program: first on the list, was the church of St. Stephen's, Stephenville, 1869. It had been under construction during Father Belanger's service; the lumber was sawn by hand.

Built in the 1800s St. Stephen's Roman Catholic Church and burned to the ground in 1960s

It is noteworthy, that a trip from Sandy Point to St. John's, in that era, took Father Sears four weeks plus one day. He made the trip by boat and skiff, on the occasion of Bishop Thomas Joseph Powers' arrival, who succeeded Bishop Mullock.

Although ill, Monsignor Sears made two trips to St. John's to promote opening up the West Coast, through road construction. He did so, between 1883 and 1885, (the year of his death). In other matters, his efforts had brought about a mail service, telegraph communications, local representation in government and he had obtained a degree of financial assistance for education. He had also been successful in getting financial assistance for the construction of carriage roads (private roads for horse drawn carriages, often connecting with a public road), particularly in the Codroy Valley. He had hoped to have main lines of roads constructed between Channel Port aux Basques and Bay of Islands, but, in this, was unsuccessful.

In 1874, our Lady of Mercy Church, Benoit's Cove, was commenced, followed by St. Patrick's Church, Bonne Bay and the Church of Holy Family, Summerside, Bay of Islands. Lumber for these churches was mainly obtained in the vicinity of what is now Broadway, Corner Brook West. In August, 1886, Father Matthew O'Rourke arrived in Sandy Point on the S. S. Curlew, to be stationed in Bay of Islands, but also served in Stephenville and Port au Port. He died in 1912. Father P. W. Brown also served in Stephenville, Bay of Islands and Bonne Bay.

The Bait Act contributed to a situation in 1888, whereby the (French) locals in Fortune Bay were obliged to proceed to the West Coast for supplies. This placed great hardships on fishermen. That delay prevented them from selling their catch to the Americans. Those Americans also had rights and were willing to pay the locals double what they were receiving from the French fleets, whose equipment was superior.

French and English warships enforced a curfew, allowing fishing only from 4 a.m. to 8 a.m. Both times were indicated by firing guns of warships. On May 7, St. George's Harbour was so full of ships of every description and nationality that the hulls of warships could not be seen. Only the lofty masts and yards were visible above the forest of smaller fishing vessels. This can scarcely be appreciated these days, when all is at a standstill, on the fishing front.

In 1886, Bishop Howley was succeeded by Bishop Neil MacNeil. He has been described as a plain, simple man (as in easy-going), with a sense of humor. He enjoyed everyday happenings, illustrated by a letter that he wrote to his sister, which reads as follows……. "My borrowed horse was lazy and stiff; the only way I could get any speed was to whip him into a gallop. It was a queer rig; the bridle was homemade; my saddle was a bag of hay fastened with rope and the stirrups were loops of cod-line. I thought the contrast too great between the gold ring, with the large amethyst stone, on my finger."

Sincerely,
Agnes Gallant

**The following is the obituary, in honor of the memory of
Agnes M. Gallant, Born: March 16, 1926. Passed June 14, 2017, Stephenville, NL**

It is with great sadness that the family of the late Agnes Mary Gallant announce her passing at the Sir Thomas Roddick Hospital in Stephenville on Wednesday, June 14, 2017 at the age of 91 years. She will be greatly missed by her fifteen nieces and nephews and a large circle of relatives and friends. Agnes graduated from the first two-year Education Program at Memorial University College in 1944 and taught school for a few years before she enrolled in the Nursing School at Glace Bay, Nova Scotia. She graduated and wrote her Nova Scotia Registered Nursing Certification. The majority of her nursing career was spent in Stephenville, first at the American Hospital at Harmon Air Force Base and then at Sir Thomas Roddick Hospital. She was predeceased by her parents Andrew Edward Gallant and Flora Anne Gallant, two brothers, Arthur Gallant (Mary) and Gerard Gallant (Nita), five sisters Mary Dolorisa Ryan (Patrick), Sarah Margaret Fitzpatrick (Gordon), Hilda Goodland (Harry), Mary Sofia Murphy (Jr.) and Mary Genevieve Pailleé (George).

JE SUIS JACKATAR – SEQUEL TO BACK OF THE POND

Right Reverend Monsignor P. F. Adams

The Right Reverend Monsignor Adams was born on the 6th of October, 1862, in Quebec and was baptized in Saint Albert's Church, on the 18th of October of that same year. He made his first Holy Communion, on 26th of April, 1875, was confirmed 16th of July, 1878 and ordained 19th of May, 1898 at St. Lawrence Seminary, Quebec.

Monsignor Adams said his first Holy Mass in St. Albert's Church, Gaspe and said his last Mass in St. Stephen's Church, on the 8th December, 1936. From that date on, until the 12th of May, 1937, his masses were said in his house. He died on Thursday, the 18th of November, 1937, (15 minutes to 9 in the morning) and was buried 20th of November, on a Saturday morning.

(Thanks to Mrs. Theresa (George) White for information and pictures of Monsignor Adams.)

JE SUIS JACKATAR – SEQUEL TO BACK OF THE POND

Naming Stephenville

Whenever the origin of the name Stephenville comes up, it almost invariably leads to a discussion on whom it was named after. In 1847, the first permanent Acadians to settle in Indian Creek, in what was to become Stephenville, were documented. They were from Margaree by the name of Marie Theothime (or Theotiste to some) LeBlanc and Felix Gallant. Marie was the daughter of Étienne LeBlanc and Ann Marie Cormier, who seasonally resided in Sandy Point. That same year, on September 3, 1847, Marie (Theotime) née LeBlanc-Gallant gave birth to a son, who was named Stephen (English for the French word Étienne). He received his name after his grandfather, (Étienne LeBlanc). **This newborn, Stephen Gallant, then became the very first Acadian settlers' child to be born at Indian Creek**. Four years later, the names Indian Creek, Indian Village, Acadian Village et al. would be combined to be called Stephenville, after that newborn, Stephen Gallant. In the year that followed, 1848, Felix and Marie took Stephen Junior to Margaree to be baptised.

At this point, there is an interesting story that has to be told. In this same year, 1847, Mr. William Hynes, from Port au Port, was walking toward Indian Head, along the shore, searching for hoop poles that were commonly used for making storage barrels. Barrel hoops were made from spruce roots, sometimes spruce saplings (small spruce trees). The roots or saplings were split down the middle, soaked in water, to soften up, then wrapped around the barrels and left there to dry. Upon drying, the roots shrunk into the barrel staves,[32] sealing them into place.

As Hynes passed near Indian Creek, he came upon a newly built cabin with smoke coming from the chimney. After making his way to the cabin, he found a woman alone and in labor. Unable to understand her French language, he set out to find help, which was

---

[32] Webster's English Dictionary, Canadian Edition, *Stave*. Strathearn Books Ltd. 1997, Toronto, Canada, Goddess and Grosser, 2002

about a mile further at the home of Susannah Hunt. They then returned to the Gallant cabin and on September 3, Marie Theothime (Theotiste) delivered Stephen, with assistance from Hunt and Hynes. By coincidence only, it turned out that Marie's husband, Felix, was also out searching for hoop poles. And to come to think of it, if they had followed Indian tradition, they could have named that baby boy 'Hoop Pole.' The gods shone down on us that day too, for, if the two Stephens hadn't surfaced at that time, the town was probably destined to be called Turnipeatersville.

I was never so aware, as I am now, just how important those hoop barrels were. Although those barrels, in my father's storehouse, were more advanced, with the metal hoops, one storage container in particular, has found a fond place in my heart. In this barrel, under some old boots and skates, I hid my school uniform in grade one. The nuns had preached to us, and warned us, that we were not allowed in school without our uniform. So, after careful calculation, I reasoned, that if my uniform was never found, I wouldn't have to go to school, ever, again. Hey, I was only six years old. I thought I was pretty darn smart, don't you think? More proof that 'we Jackatars are not as stun as we looks, eh!'

When Felix, and his wife Marie, went to Margaree for their son's baptism, they told others of their newfound homestead. When they returned to Indian Creek, friends and family followed. Among the first to arrive were Marie's parents and members of her extended family. There was Étienne's brother, Celestine, with his wife Marie Modeste née Cormier and their family. And there were the two families of Constant Aucoin and his wife Marceline née LeBlanc, as well as Tassien Aucoin and Margaret Aurelie née LeBlanc. Others soon followed. Tassien was a crew member and probably a master on one of those schooners that was used to bring these settlers from Margaree to Bay St. George.

Edward Gaudon was born in France, but in 1848, he was on a French fishing boat at Red Island, near Bay St. George. As others, like the Russell's, had done before him, Edward jumped ship and was soon pursued by French officials. To avoid the inevitable punishment that he would face if caught, Edward hid out in the woods, in what is now the town of Stephenville. In the spirit of humor, Edward later explains how he convinces his pursuers that he is, indeed, not hiding in the woods behind Indian Creek. "Oh, non Monsieur Mounties, je suis Edouard et je peux vous donner une bonne garantie que je ne me cache pas derriere cette souche én bois, derriére Le Ruisseau Indian." In English, this would read something like, "Oh, no Mr. Mountie, I can promise you, faithfully, that I am not hiding behind this stump, behind Indian Creek." Eventually, Edward made contact with the local settlers. A year later, he married Marie Ann Madore of Sandy Point and he also became **another**, among the settlers. Settlers to Newfoundland's Acadia set to work clearing, building, hunting and fishing. They also farmed with the help of their animals and equipment that they had brought from Cape Breton. Soon, these pastoral settlers had their land cultivated, their crops planted and their homes, barns and sheds built. Among their animals, the sheep alone provided food and clothing. Looms and other items for weaving were very important and useful. Making blankets and clothes out of the wool from the sheep was yet another skill that they had mastered on their own.

Circa 1955 – Washing Wool
R–L: Mary née Burns-Ryan, Ursula née Ryan-Schumph. Left of Ursula, drum for heating water, Center, two wash tubs; in front, wool strewn about, in bags and loose. The wool was dried on flakes and then carded and spun into yarn using a spinning wheel.

JE SUIS JACKATAR – SEQUEL TO BACK OF THE POND

Alexis Jesso (Jesseaume) and Anne Marie Young (Lejeune) settled down in the Kippens area in 1842, with Peter, their newborn. Between 1848 and 1849, Raymond and Esther née Bourgeois also arrived with their family. There were still others who were leaving Chéticamp as well, like Jean and Pelagie Cormier Gaudet. They settled in Kippens in 1850, along with family members. Pierre Doucet and Marie Cormier also settled in, after they were married.

Around that same time, but a little further to the East, a married couple from Margaree, Helen LeBlanc and Luc Benoit, were building their home at Indian Creek. Dominic LeBlanc, son of Étienne, had married Helen (Penil) Penney from Sandy Point and was keeping close ties with both their friends and family members in Sandy Point, Indian Creek and Chéticamp. The brothers, Celestine and Étienne had large families, some of whom were young adults that were left behind, in Margaree. In time, these young adults also began arriving in Indian Creek and soon married into the local expanding population. As these Acadians became firmly established, they began to bond with the earth, in their new found Acadie.

JE SUIS JACKATAR – SEQUEL TO BACK OF THE POND

First European 'Arrivals'

Philippe and Suzanne Messervey were the first European settlers to arrive at Sandy Point in 1791. They were followed by more English and Channel Islanders. People of mixed Mi'kmaq and French heritage were the next to arrive. Being predominantly Catholic, several of those settler families lived on a section of land that was mapped as Jacotar Point. To this day, virtually every Mi'kmaq is a baptized Christian, baptized into the Roman Catholic Church.[33]

Jacotar is a derogatory term, an ethnic and racial slur that was commonly used by many Newfoundlanders. Because there were a larger number of Mi'kmaq, as well as French and Indian mix, among the settlers in the Bay, the phrase 'Land of the Jackatars' became quite common, when describing people from the Bay St. George district, especially those on the Southwest Coast.

I'm sure a distinguished author, like Farley Mowat[34], wasn't being complementary when he wrote the following about Jackatars and gypsies, after he visited Bay St. George. "They were a category of people", he said "whose social status might be compared to that of gypsies. They were generally rather small and wiry folk, dark hair and dark complexion." Preconceived notions of Jackatars have, especially in past years, caused undue hardship to our ancestors. As Maura Hanrahan wrote, in her essay 'Beothuk Romanticism and Mi'kmaq Realities'[35], the derogatory word 'Jackatar' was bandied about for decades and the Mi'kmaq were, without a shred of evidence, blamed for, among other crimes, killing off the Beothuks. No wonder so many Mi'kmaq reacted by hiding or trying to hide their identity.

---

[33] Carolyn Girard, *The Catholic Registrar, June 30, 2010*
[34] Farley Mowat, *The Farfarers, Before the Norse,* 1998, p. 345
[35] www. theindependent.ca>beothuk

JE SUIS JACKATAR – SEQUEL TO BACK OF THE POND

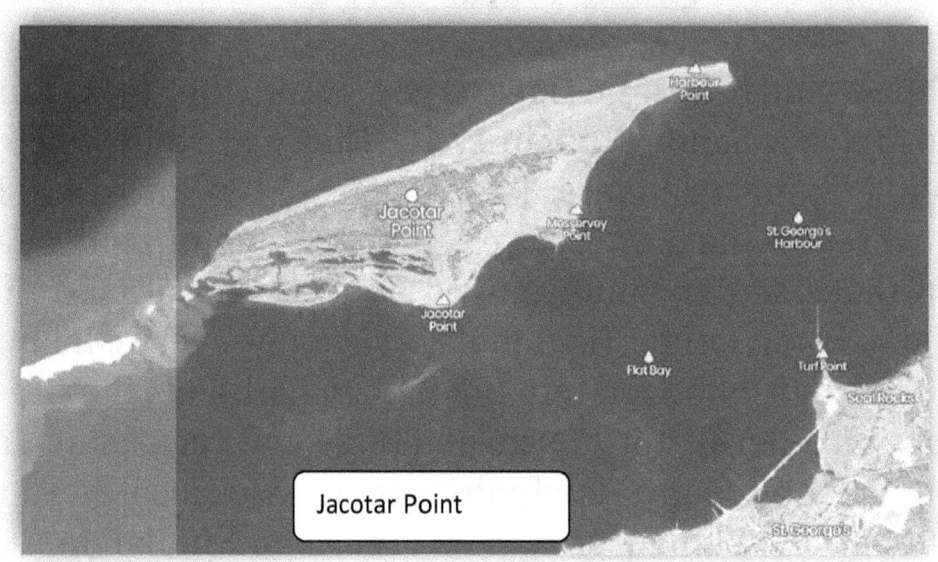

Black Bank

Black Bank – St. George's, Newfoundland

Sand dunes are large masses of sand that have been built up by the wind, the flow of water or both. Examples are the Sahara Dessert and beaches i.e. Black Bank. The sand dunes are vulnerable to dirt bikes and quads, which leave beaches at high risk of ersosion.

A good natured way of referring to, or distinguishing one community from another, was to label each according to their activities and/or their surroundings. For example, people from Sandy Point, Stephenville Crossing and St. George's were called 'sand scratchers'; people from the farming community of Stephenville were called "turnip eaters' and those of Port au Port were nicknamed 'herring chokers' because of the vibrant fishery.

As the community of Stephenville underwent its growing pains, the number of sawmills increased. The trapping of fur animals and hunting of wildlife in the backwoods provided revenue and food. Further processing of abundant resources, like cow's milk and sheep's wool for instance, took place in a local butter factory and a carding mill. Soon, with the completion of the railway in 1898, root crops were sent to major centers across the Island. The number of general stores began to increase in the local area. Employment opportunities were finally available in the North Eastern States, on Anticosti Island and in the Atlantic Provinces i.e. for lumberjacks. On the Island itself, there were two new paper mills and various mining opportunities. In addition, following the introduction of the railway, big game hunting and fly-fishing increased the need for experienced guides and outfitters, a job that could easily be filled by the locals, especially the aboriginals in the area.

Religious guidelines were very strict, and those who did convert to a different religion were sometimes ignored, or even disowned by their families. We must note that in the early settler days, the gene pool was very small and it only stands to reason that there were very few suitors. That prompted some of the young adults to take a tantalizing look at the forbidden fruit, whether that be a ravishing Roman or a predatory Protestant.

Now is the perfect time to talk about the apron games. But before I recite these two stories about a few of our Acadian friends, I want to explain the following lyric. 'Me fadder he was orange[36] and me mudder she was green.' These two colors orange and green date

---

[36] www. en.wikipedia.org.wiki *principality of orange,*

back to the 16th and 17th hundreds, when the Protestant Irish were under the rule of King William III of Scotland, Ireland and England. In the Battle of the Boyne, near Dublin, William III of Orange, a Protestant, defeated the armies of King James II, a Roman Catholic. In addition, in 1789, the Irish Catholics rose up against the British (Protestants), in defiance of an unwritten law that forbid the color green to be worn by the Catholics. The British saw such a move as being rebellious. If the Catholics wore green clothes or shamrocks, it could even lead to their death by hanging etc. And so it follows, that to say "me fodder he was orange" is the same as: my father was of the Protestant faith and to say "me mudder she was green" is the same as: my mother was of the Roman Catholic faith.

The Irish folk song 'The Orange and the Green' is a humorous way to tell the history of that turbulent time, and how it was the biggest mix-up that they had ever seen. The song describes a man's ordeal, trials and tribulations, as he grew up with a Catholic mother (Green), and a Protestant father (Orange). The song was written by Anthony Murphy of Liverpool, and recorded by The Irish Rovers and other musicians. The song is worth listening to.

<u>The Orange and the Green</u>

Oh, it is the biggest mix-up that you have ever seen.
My father, he was Orange and me mother, she was Green.

My father was an Ulster man, proud Protestant was he.
My mother was a Catholic girl, from County Cork was she.
They were married in two churches, lived happily enough,
Until the day that I was born and things got rather tough.

Oh, it is the biggest mix-up that you have ever seen.
My father, he was Orange and me mother, she was Green.

Baptized by Father Riley, I was rushed away by car,
To be made a little Orangeman, me father's shining star.
I was christened "David Anthony," but still, inspite of that,
To me father, I was William, while my mother called me Pat.

Oh, it is the biggest mix-up that you have ever seen.
My father, he was Orange and me...

Story #1 Let the Apron Games begin:

The following story demonstrates that in spite of religious differences, true love can sometimes conquer all. Interestingly, there was one particular case of a Protestant fellow from Seal Rocks, near St. Georges, who sparked the interest of a young Catholic girl from Barachois Brook. Despite warnings from their parents, this couple pursued a relationship.

To facilitate the romance, the sisters of the young girl hung an apron on the outside of the front door of their farmhouse, as a symbol that the old lady wasn't around.

The belle was the daughter of an Irish farming family from the Avalon Peninsula, and the beau was the son of the fellow of the Loyal Orangeman's Lodge (LOL). Love prevailed. The couple eventually married and raised a large family of maudits [37]gamines[38] and god-loves. Of the many obstacles in their way, who would think that such a mundane item, as an apron, could break through the barriers of segregation? Many daughters and sons were disowned by their families if they married outside their religion.

---

[37] www.en.wiktionary.org *Maudit*
[38] www.en.wiktionary.org *Gamine*

Story #2 – with a twist of conscience.

One of the elders, prominent in the community, was renowned for her love of playing cards, in particular, one hundred and twenty (120). Card games were a frequent pastime, in most cases played almost every night of the week, especially in winter time, in alternate houses. On one particular occasion, this lady was having a seemingly lucky streak. However, the next day, the euphoria of winning was dampened by her realization that she had purposely cheated. At some point, before the game started, she had 'picked the pack', and

kept the ace of hearts in her apron. Her deep Roman Catholic religious upbringing caused her to become overwhelmed with guilt. Once she processed what she had done, she felt the need to confess and atone for her sin. Without hesitation, she walked from Kippens, three miles, to the church. Relieved, she found a priest there and asked if she could go to confession. When the priest asked her why, she answered "because I hid the ace of hearts in my apron." The priest assured her that she had not sinned, that there was no money involved, and that card playing was just a game. Further to that, the priest admitted, other members of the clergy had told him, for a fact, that even the Bishop, Bishop O'Reilly, had been prone to cheating at one hundred and twenty (120). "And now my child", said the priest, "go and sin no more."

Cupids Converts

Cupid, it appeared, was an agnostic. He fired off his arrows indiscriminately, the result of which, couples of different faiths had to make a compromise. A cupid's convert was someone who changed his/her religion to accommodate their betrothed. With a limited number of families, there were few marital prospects, of the same faith, among the community. But, there was always someone willing and eager to jump the fence, so-to-speak. Enter, our friend Cupid! To a Protestant looking for a partner, a Catholic was definitely cuter and more appealing. To a ravishing Roman, a Protestant appeared prettier and more proper. And from these came the terms of endearment:

(1) I likes you me, and I dies at you!

(2) I finds you cute, but you're brā..zen, you.

(3) "If you wants to kiss I, kiss I, Don't lick I all over."

(4) I shivers when I tinks about you, me.

(5) God bless your cotton socks.

(6) Ow ye getting' on dere, old cocky?

In research records dating 1849, Acadian researcher Thomas LeBlanc (White) recorded that Dominic was the son of Étienne (Stephen) LeBlanc (White) and Anne Marie Cormier, and married Helen Penney in 1850. Helen and her sister Suzanne were the first Penney surnames to surface on church documents in St. George's Inner Bay. Suzanne Penney converted to Catholicism to marry

William Madore in St. George's in 1855. It is quite possible that her sister Helen was also a convert when she married Dominic LeBlanc (White). Reverend Belanger, the French priest, more than likely officiated at marriages for both Helen and Suzanne.

It is believed by, some, that Belanger may have misunderstood or inadvertently misspelled the surname Penil, which because of its pronunciation, later got recorded as Penney. Once the two Penil girls were married, as the times dictated, they dropped their maiden name and took on their husband's surname, explaining why the changes might not have become an issue. This was also a time when there were two distinct languages, French and English, in common use and overlapping. For example, it was an everyday occurrence for the French to insert an English word into a sentence, if they didn't know the French word or if they weren't getting their message across.

Chapter 7

Naming Family Members

As the Mi'kmaq assimilated into the Acadian Culture, both had to adjust to each other's lifestyle and customs. Traditional, English given names and surnames were foreign to the Mi'kmaq. Customs varied among different tribes, but some chose names that related to their birth, in many cases, nature. For example, if a child was born in the very early hours of the morning, she might be given the name Dawn, as my daughter was. Another notable fact is that family and given names are often reversed by the Mi'kmaq, for example Sylvester Joe. Often times, they appear to have no surnames, rather two first names instead, like James John.

French Acadians were choosing the most common Christian names, like Joe and Mary, for their newborns. To add to the confusion, some families named all their daughters Mary, followed by a second name, i.e. Mary Louise. Some even gave their boys the middle name Mary or Marie, etc.

Other names were chosen from a Christian Calendar, the only calendar, I remember, ever having in our home. If a name chosen by the parents suggested anything other than Christian, or the priest baptising the child didn't like the name chosen by the parents, for any reason, he would choose one that he preferred. Again, almost invariably, a Christian choice, like Joe or John was given; girls were most often given the names Mary or Marie.

The Mi'kmaq and French Acadians alike, started to attach the father's first name after the child's first name. To add to the confusion, there were scores of the same surnames, such as the Whites (LeBlanc) and the Benoits. So, it followed that those traditions, like adding the father's first name after the child's, would eliminate some of the confusion. Joe, son of Maxim White, might be Joe à Maxim; Joe, son of Venna White could become Joe Venna and Joe, son of Telesphore could be referred to as Joe of Telesphore or the equivalent of.

Another means of remembering a person was by association, to attach an identifying feature, either before or after the first name. Examples were:

(1)   Jigger Joe, who was known for his fly-fishing techniques.
(2)   Joe Paint, the artist.
(3)   Taxi Joe, who drove taxi.
(4)   There was even a laughing Charlie, who was always pleasant, positive and happy go-lucky.

As well, the Mi'kmaq had another unique way of honouring their fellow man. Sometimes, they would add the name of someone they admired to the birth name. For example, someone, like Sylvester Joe, might have gained a great respect for Williams Epps Cormack when they traversed the country together. Had Sylvester Joe fathered a son, after the expedition, he could show that respect in a very meaningful way, by adding Cormack's first or middle name to his son's name. Let's say he names his son Brook; he could add William after Brook and so his son's name would become Brook William or William Brook.

Sometimes, to further distinguish one from another, the Mi'kmaq or French Acadian would identify the women by their husband's first name, such as Nita à Paddy (my parents), Lena Luke or Rita Joe (my aunts and uncles). Women have been forever losing their identities once they marry, at which time their maiden name is dropped and their husband's last name is taken. For example, my maiden name is Benoit, but dropped when I married a Penney. Now, my name is Mercedes Penney. If I allow this common practice to identify me, I feel as if I'm forfeiting my identity. When the name Benoit comes up, no one looks to me to confirm a connection; in a similar way, when the name Penney arises, people automatically make the connection between that name and me.

Remembering Siki

Siki Bennett, St. George's
Winner 10-mile Road Race
Grand Falls, Newfoundland.
Circa 1933

JE SUIS JACKATAR – SEQUEL TO BACK OF THE POND

Jackatar Poster Boy – Siki

When the American Base opened in Stephenville, Newfoundland, in 1941, Franklin D. Roosevelt, Commander and Chief, was very concerned with the morale of the troops. He brought together, among other organizations, an entertainment division called the U.S.O. (United Service Organization)[39] to lift the spirits of their service people and their families. During the years of its stay in Stephenville and up to its closure in 1966, the Harmon Base featured a host of entertainment celebrities such as Bob Hope, Marilyn Monroe, Frank Sinatra, Jayne Mansfield, Johnny Cash and Kitty Wells, to name some.

Another consideration for the morale of the troops was that of sports and fitness such as baseball, basketball, track and field and in the winter months, skating and skiing. Meanwhile, across the Bay, in the community of Seal Rocks, (one of the oldest of three settlements that now make up the town of St. George's), a local legend was going to have an entertaining influence on those recent American arrivals.

Richard (Siki) Bennett (Benoit)

Richard Bennett (Benoit, nicknamed Siki) born December 11, 1909, was one of fourteen children of John Edward Benoit and Elizabeth (Betsy) Young-Benoit. In the 1940s Siki met Mary Collier and started a family in St. George's.

Among his numerous accolades, he had built an outdoor arena in his home town of St. George's. He became very involved with the youth, in particular, in sports such as hockey and boxing. He helped to organize local hockey teams, looked after the rinks ice-surface, arranged many of the games and did some of the refereeing.

---

[39] Mercedes Benoit-Penney, *Back of the Pond, Revised Edition*, McMinnville, TN. Page 73, 2018

He also had a keen interest in active sports such as snowshoeing and long-distance running. In August 2007, the residents of St. George's decided to honor Bennett (Siki) by renaming their Rec Plex after him. Since then, the building carries the name Siki Bennett Memorial Arena.

NOTE: [The French Acadian name 'Benoit' was changed to Bennett, in almost all cases, by the English clergy and officials, while we were under British rule and even after Confederation].

Once hired to work on Ernest Harmon Air Force Base, his employer began to realize Siki's many talents. One, that was widely rumoured, was his ability to put down an exceptional sheet of ice; another, that he was well versed in the art of wood working. Realizing Siki's skills, the Americans assigned him to the Woodwork Hobby Shop. There, he showed an amazing talent for making wooden picture frames for religious and local icons. This was a time of ecclesiastical (religious) fervor in the communities and his contribution to Christian Art didn't go unnoticed.

When I grew up in the 1950s and 1960s, I remember that every Catholic home I was into had framed icons of religion, royalty and/or politicians. It was a sign of the times, as I alluded to in my previous book <u>Back of the Pond</u>. My birthday present, a picture of the Blessed Virgin Mary on page 81 of the <u>Revised Edition</u>, can attest to that. It was a time of tribute to such figures as the Pope, the Holy Family, the Royal Family, Mosey Burns (Murrin) and in later years Joey Smallwood. The art gave the Town of Stephenville a sense of belonging, of community.

Growing up in Seal Rocks, a small coastal community of approximately 250 residents, Siki, like his other childhood friends, was used to the simple things in life. Most families lived off the land, farmed, hunted and/or fished for survival. Siki lived a hearty lifestyle, working hard and finding ways to pass the time. Later in life, he still participated in Marathon races, competing in central Newfoundland, with the best of them.

JE SUIS JACKATAR – SEQUEL TO BACK OF THE POND

Being around home-made rinks for some time, with his involvement in ice sports, such as hockey, 'Siki's practice soon makes perfect,' as the age old saying goes. Again, the Americans approached him to take on the task of maintaining an ice rink on the base premises. Carpenters were assigned to build a proper frame and structure. Electricians put lines of lights (suspended from poles) across the rink, bringing something very new to the area, evening and night-time skating. Then Siki, as usual, performed his magic. After preparing the base of the rink with sawdust, he proceeded to put down a sheet of ice, with water that was hosed from a nearby hydrant. Keep in mind that this all took place in the 1940s, before the time of electricity in Newfoundland. This skating rink was a big deal. In fact, it wasn't until 1956 that the first illuminated indoor skating rink appeared on the West Coast of the Island.

Coming from a large family, idleness and restlessness were probably never qualities that described Siki or his siblings, certainly not the definition of lazy or indolent, which appears in some dictionaries. Here, in South Western Newfoundland, most of us use the term idleness to describe a person who has a good sense of humor. Siki and his brother, Aussie, loved practical jokes and they would do almost anything, outside the norm, to attract someone's attention. They were 'idle, humorous and mischievous' characters, as was relayed by Bob Mercer, another former resident of Seal Rocks.

Aussi, whose family lived close to Mercer's Pond, near his home, happened to notice a group of young girls from St. Michael's College, St. George's. They had come to the pond to skate on the wind-swept, clear ice. They were accompanied by their escorts, the Sisters of Mercy, who were responsible for running all aspects of the school, in particular, supervision.

So it was, on that particular day, when Aussi came upon this giggling gaggle of frolicking females, that he just couldn't resist the urge to perform and impress such a welcomed distraction. He knew that the ice surface had several gaping holes, where blocks of ice had been removed from the pond by local fishermen, holes big enough for a man to fall into. Two of those holes were approximately thirty feet apart and in perfect view of the female spectators. Aussi proceeded to strip off his clothes, down to his Stanfield Long Johns, shouted such words as "I'll be back soon" and then jumped into the nearby hole. The onlookers, in awe, were shocked that he had just disappeared before their very eyes. They didn't realize that Aussi was swimming, underneath the ice, to another opening. After an agonizing minute or so, Aussi popped up from a second hole, like a seal coming up for air.

Anything that attracted female attention was not beyond the realm of Aussi, or his brothers, it seemed, anything to impress the girls. The stunt that Aussi pulled that day was well rewarded, in his mind, I'm sure, but would be considered risky by most others standards. It, I'd dare to say, was very amusing to the young women, as it elicited positive reactions like giggling and laughing, not to mention what images were conjured up in their minds by the sight of this water-soaked, corpse-like specimen of a man in his underwear. This was just one day in the life of Aussi, Siki's brother.

The family of Bennett's (Benoit's) were direct descendants of Mi'kmaq who came to the island from Nova Scotia in the early 18th Century (1700). Twenty such families came from Cape Breton to Bay St. George and settled in Seal Rocks under the auspices of the Newfoundland and Nova Scotia governments. After being in the area for a number of years, some of those families left the Bay area and went to settle in Conne River, others to Crow Gulch. By the 1930s, there were still some members (descendants) of those families, such as the Joe family and the Paul family, left in Barachois

Aussie (Bennett) Benoit
Born August 17, 1918
Died July 17, 1999

Brook. Siki Bennett's family members were some of the direct descendants of the original Mi'kmaq.

Healing Power

Joe Paul, a native Mi'kmaw, was believed to be somewhat of a medicine man with healing powers for doing good. One day, it was told to me, Joe Paul was on his way home, when it started to pour rain. He approached the home of a Ms. Harnett and asked if he might stay awhile. She called out for him to come in, but was unable to get up from lying down, because she was having back problems. Joe got them a cup of tea and asked again how she was feeling. He suggested that he might be able to relieve some of her pain. Joe helped Ms. Harnett to a chair and proceeded to massage her back and shoulders. She felt immediate relief and the pain gradually left.

A Mr. Cashin relayed a similar story about his father. Although reluctant, at first, to allow a Jack-o-tar into his home, there came a time when the pain got so unbearable that he put aside all inhibitions and allowed a call to be made for Joe to intercede. The same type of hands-on-technique was used on Cashin as Ms. Harnett. Cashin felt immediate relief. He was so grateful; he told Joe that he was welcome back into his house anytime. This was a time, long before chiropractors and massage therapists. The fact that Joe Paul had the knowledge to heal is very astounding, considering he didn't have any schooling, apart from what was taught to him by his elders.

JE SUIS JACKATAR – SEQUEL TO BACK OF THE POND

Joe's Bachelor Pad

Joe Paul (born around 1890) lived up [40]Barachois Brook, near St. George's, in his Bachelor Pad, in the most basic of accommodations. He lived in a small cabin, hunting and gathering, as was typical of other nomads, for furs and food. In the winter months though, as was dictated by Raymond Leroux of Seal Rocks, Joe Paul lived in a cellar. His dwelling was based on the principle of a Beaver Lodge; body heat would be preserved. Strange how all beavers knew this, but few of us honkies did. The lower-level entrance gradually sloped down and then upward to reach the living area. His home was constructed in a secluded place, on the bank of the brook, reached by walking along the Main Gut, up to Barachois Brook.

There was a tree growing up the side of the riverbank, with its lower branches cut off. If you stepped on the right tree branch, approximately eight feet down, you could expose a hole in the bank, which was the entrance to his abode. The whole structure was far enough into the ground to be below the frost line. With the ceiling supported by wooden beams, animal pelts for cover and for lining the floor and Joe's own body heat, it would have been quite comfortable. In the same way a cellar works, it offered to protect Joe from the freezing temperatures of late fall and winter months.

The upper level of his dwelling was big enough to crawl into, but not high enough to stand upright in, unless, of course, you were a short person. Here, Joe Paul could perform menial tasks, such as skinning the animals he caught, preparing traps, eating, sleeping etc. There was always an inherent danger, though, of bringing a woman in, in the off chance that she might try to change the furniture around. And so, it may have been inevitable. Did Joe Paul indeed, remain a bachelor?

---

[40] En.wikipedia.org>wiki> *Barachois*

Captain Tulk

Another member of the Joe family was believed, by some, to have supernatural powers. A resident of Barachois Brook, Captain Tulk, was eking out a living as a fisherman. Living near the coast, Tulk owned a schooner, his pride and joy, off which he fished and spent most of his time, when the weather proved fit. Tulk would haul up his little schooner in Barachois Brook, a safe haven, until weather permitted, to put it back in the water.

One fine morning in spring, a young Mi'kmaw girl from the Joe family, knocked on Tulk's door, looking to borrow a cup of sugar. Tulk rudely dismissed the girl, telling her he had no time for such trivial matters and he had more important things on his mind, like launching his schooner. "Maybe you're spending just a-little-too much time launching your boat, Sir," said the girl and then she left the premises.

For days, Tulk continued to have problems and further delays. His friends and neighbours thought that the problems continued as a result of a curse that Mary Joe, the Mi'kmaw woman, had put on him. Finally, the day came to launch his schooner. The weather was right; Tulk had taken care of the technical problems; all seemed in order when he embarked on his fishing trip. But still, Captain Tulk continued to have problems with his schooner, on and off as the weeks went by, until finally the schooner and its cargo sunk. He and his crew escaped the peril. So, it looked, indeed, 'like the bad luck baby put the jinks on (He)'.

Chapter 8

Newcomers Take Root

The Serle family was believed to be the first European Settlers in Western Newfoundland. Originally from the Channel Islands in the English Channel (off the French Coast of Normandy), it is interesting to take note of a remarkable French widow by the name of Ann Serle Hulan. In the Three Rivers area in South-Western Newfoundland, she had taken the prerogative of planting seven different varieties of potatoes. In doing so, she was less affected by the potato blight of the early 1800s. Ann was recognized by the Maritime Agricultural Magazine for her ingenuity, once again showing that education is not always school grown.

Paling Fence

The Acadians of the Stephenville area showed the same ingenuity. They had the tradition of bringing root crop seed into the country in springtime. In the bogs they would plant vegetables like turnip, cabbage, carrot and potatoes, vegetables that they regularly ate. The peat bogs were rich in black ground. When these hunters, fishers, trappers and/or wood cutters went back into the country in the fall, they would have a fresh crop waiting for them. They protected their crops from the animals by a paling fence, which they built out of nearby wood.

The Acadian lifestyle, with its deep connection to the land, caused these pioneers to acquire independence and the ability to be inventive. What we take for granted today, the Acadians had to make for themselves. In around 1850, when these settlers first came to the local area and to Stephenville, they saw great potential in the forest, the rich soil, a large fresh water pond 'Stephenville Pond,' (not to be confused with Noel's Pond), and the nearby ocean. With these resources that were available, they were able to craft all the necessities of life.

These newcomers lived and prospered peacefully among their neighbors, the Mi'kmaq, in their new surroundings. All the while, the Acadians and the Mi'kmaq assisted each other. They grew the crops they needed in the fertile soil that was abundant there. They planted fruit trees, such as plum, cherry and apple that some believed were brought over from France and they grew various evergreens. In the springtime, the Mi'kmaq taught the French how to tap the maple trees for syrup. They each shared knowledge of homemade remedies from the weeds, shrubs and trees, such as poultices, plasters, tonics, drinks etc., to treat scores of health problems.

Acadian communities were the most self-sustaining in Newfoundland. They kept animals such as sheep, cows, pigs, and chickens – whatever they needed to supply food for the year around. Wild animals, small and big game, like rabbit and caribou were plentiful and used for making clothes, as well as for food. Nothing was thrown away. All materials had a purpose and at the end of the day, these people supplied everything they needed, from skis to wagons, to a reel of thread. One tidbit of information that solidifies the theory that the Acadians were industrious and patient was a story told to me by my father. He told us of a gentleman (I wish I could remember his name), who made sewing needles back in his day. It took him, dad said, two days to make one needle and he sold them two for a cent and that's not a word of a lie.

Back then, before governing bodies controlled our every move and action, these pioneers had paved a rich and bountiful pathway for us to follow, a path rich in natural resources. They did so, by using their common sense and their minds to solve problems. They made furniture, soap and candles, to name a few. Numerous varieties of fish were abundant and herring was a perfect fertilizer for their gardens. They built their homes from the forests around them and they enjoyed a hearty and healthy lifestyle, were busy all the time, but happy that way. They had friends and family close by and they got together often to party, with food, music and dance. I'm learning to never underestimate the ingenuity of the Jackatars. For example, in my grandmother's time, it was fashionable for women to wear high heels inside their galoshes in wintertime. One lady in particular was trying to avoid a wardrobe malfunction. After consulting with her older daughter, she finally came up with a solution to her dilemma.

The lady I speak of didn't own a pair of shoes with high heels, so she diligently put her mind and hands to work. She custom cut two pieces of turnip in the shape and height she preferred and placed them securely in the heels of her boots. That gave her the extra elevation and elation, no doubt that she was looking for. Then, at Mass the coming Sunday, she was able to strut her stuff, along with the best of them. Not only the righteous, but also the social high point of the week, was Mass on Sunday.

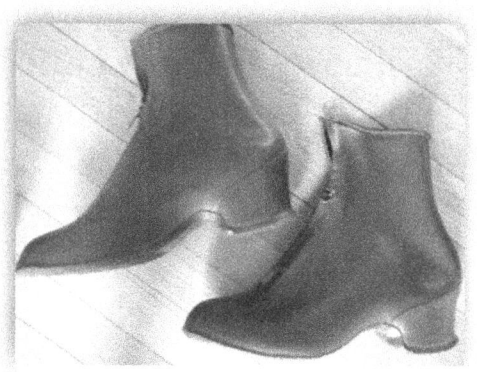
Golashes

For entertainment, Acadians made their own musical instruments. There were those among them who took an interest in making fiddles, violins and/or guitars, but flutes or whistles were more commonly crafted. The Acadians played the spoons, because these items were most always near at hand and with practice, they became a widely used and artful instrument.

Another means of entertainment was to play the ugly stick. These musical instruments were commonly self-made with an old mop, broom or smooth pole approximately a person's height.

Ugly Stick

Attachments were added to form the caricature of an ugly or comical character. Traditionally, such a stick was fashioned out of useless items such as felt roofing-tins and tin cans, attached up and down the pole. You can add any color noise makers, screws, nails, decorations, bells, beer caps, etc., anything your heart desires, to form the features.

Typically, no two ugly sticks were alike. The musical device was endowed with an old rubber boot for the base and was played with a drum stick or similar substitute. The idea was to hit the stick in various spots to create distinctive sounds, while holding the ugly stick with one hand, the drumstick with the other. The ugly stick was often lifted up and down so that the boot would hit the floor in a rhythmic fashion, while the musician struck the noise makers to enhance the sound, to beat the band, as the old saying goes.

Adding to their pastimes, the Acadians loved flying kites. These skilled pioneers formed the cross shape for the kite with carved wooden sticks. They then strengthened the kite by reinforcing the perimeter with string. Once the frame was made, newspaper, wallpaper, brown wrapping paper, or other suitable materials on hand, would be precisely cut to fit and fasten to the frame with a flour and water paste. I was surprised to learn that Nova Scotia had, in recent years, celebrated an 'Acadian Tide Kite Days Festival', that last took place in 2017, from June to September.

Kite

With the elders, there was a great deal of square dancing, step dancing and old-fashioned waltzing. On rare occasions, when there were no instruments around, some members of the community had the ability to perform the art of chinning, mouthing a melodious tune, one that was vibrant enough to dance a jig or reel to. Emile Benoit was a perfect example in his tune, 'Arriving in St. John's'. Coaxing was a significant part of Acadian culture and is still prevalent today. For example, in order to get someone talking about a story or an event, you had to relentlessly flatter them. Tell them you heard what a great story teller they were; that they were the best in the area and convince them until they gave in. Coaxing was done to get others to follow you in some communal activity, like going to the garden party, playing a tune, or playing a game or other methods of entertainment. Coaxing is trying to convince someone to do something that they are initially not interested in doing. It is using flattery and persistence to talk them over, if necessary, to convince them to agree to your proposal.

Another form of entertainment, prevalent among Acadians was 'Acting the Fool'. In humor, an individual would tell a self-ridiculing story or joke as in 'I'm not as stun as I looks' or 'My 'god love' told me I'm not so god love after all.' The important thing to realize is that it was all told in the spirit of fun.

A unique game, Jack Knife, was played with a pocket knife, which most boys carried and was probably considered a necessity in those years. The game, played by both young and adults, was to hand-flip a pocket knife off different parts of the hand, the fingers for instance, and to successfully flip and stick the knife into the ground. Rules of the game differed a little, depending on where you lived, (rules passed on from one community to another got distorted sometimes), but basically the one who could do the most successful flips, would win the game. There were also games like soccer and stilt-walking. They enjoyed a fundamental form of baseball, one that was played with a tennis ball. Marbles, hopscotch, making cuppies or playing house and skipping rope, all were common.

Stilt-walking

A fun activity, which was told to me by a man from Seal Rocks, was to crush milk cans, one under each foot. If crushed right, the cans would attach to the feet without falling off. This new footwear was noisy and cumbersome, a fun activity for children. To add a little imagination to the play, the young children at Seal Rocks would pretend they were animals and wander around making animal noises, most often pretending they were wearing horse shoes, thus the neighing sound of horses. They also tied a spruce or var tree branch behind them, one that was large enough to kick up lots of dust, and they would pretend they were members of a posse, playing cowboys. They would then gallop through the town on their imaginative horses. This game was played in other communities as well, before television was introduced into the homes.

First Passenger Train, 1898

After the running of the first passenger train across the whole Newfoundland Island in 1898, new opportunities opened for work, on and off the island. The able-bodied men and women of Bay St. George, being tillers of the soil, were used to hard work. And now, they had a scheduled transportation service to the Maritimes, Mainland Canada and to the United States. By way of train and the North Sydney ship-crossings from Port aux Basques, they could travel more freely than ever before. The people of Bay St. George were closest to these opportunities and soon availed of them.

For possibly the first time, seasonal workers travelled to the New England States and/or to the Maritimes, where most worked in camp jobs as wood-cutters. In Maine, there were a number of newsprint paper mills that drew seasonal workers. Likewise, good employment opportunities were available in Maritime shipping, in Halifax and Sydney. Some men chose to work in mines; others went to the lumber camps in New Brunswick and/or Maine, where work was more plentiful. Some women also travelled away for work, but their numbers were much smaller. Anticosti Island, Inverness,

Margaree and Little Bras d'Or were also frequented by Newfoundlanders who travelled seasonally for work. This was before the opening of the American Base and for most, their first opportunity to make cash in hand.

Arsene V. Gallant (May 17, 1889 – November 26, 1971) was known to have traveled from Bay St. George to Maine and surrounding areas, as a wood contractor in pulp and paper mills. To those of us who grew up in Stephenville or frequented his store (for ice-cream in our school days), we called him A. V.; few of us knew his name. He was a shrewd entrepreneur who learned the lumber woods trade and opened up his own camp in Gallants, northeast of Stephenville. That community is believed, by some, to be named after him.

Arsene Victor Gallant
Died November 26, 1971, Age 82

Sarah Alice (AuCoin) Gallant
(Wife of Arsene Victor Gallant)
Died March 17, 1958, Age 66

JE SUIS JACKATAR – SEQUEL TO BACK OF THE POND

In wintertime, the Acadians wore Mukluks, traditionally made of sealskin or other animal hides, like cowhide, moose or caribou. These boots normally rose as far as the ankle and were worn with heavy warm liners, made from any number of fur bearing animals, such as fox, bears, beavers etc.

Mukluks

Before the days of tumble dryers, the Acadians depended on the ever-present clothesline, to dry their wash. First of all, they made their scrub boards out of hardwood, i.e., birch or maple. Before they had water in their homes, they would wash their clothes in nearby streams or ponds, using scrub boards with homemade lye soap. Scrubbing their laundry against the ridges of the board made the clothes cleaner than washing machines do today, with their agitators intact.

Their clotheslines were attached to a fixed structure, such as a house or a tree and then to a vertical pole some forty or fifty feet away. The rope could be gotten from the fisherman's supply and it could be lowered and raised by a notched longer, sometimes affectionately called a 'headache stick'. The clothesline made me remember that the women in our lane, where we lived on James Street, (then called West Street), would be seen occasionally wearing step-ins (women's underpants) on their heads. (Oh, Shades of Peyton Place!). This was a common trend when they mixed bread, to avoid hair falling into the mix.

Women and the occasional man, (like my father) mixed bread almost every day, because of the large families. Ours was a family of four boys and four girls. Altogether, my father, Paddy Benoit, with his two brothers, Luke and Joe and their wives Agnita (Mom) Lena and Rita, who lived nearby on James Street, had a combined total of 29 children. That's a lot of homemade bread and a lot of clothes-washing. Thank God, by then, they had advanced a little to the old portable wringer washers. Still, there was little time to take the step-ins off (the head that is). No wonder the women would inadvertently, on occasion, go outside the home to perform some chore or other, still wearing the trendy apparel.

Snowshoes, that these Acadians industriously sculpted, were an essential piece of footwear in winter. Strapped onto the Mukluk, it provided a practical means of travel, in a time when there were no roads, except for the paths that they, with their animals, carved out themselves. All purpose play sleds were another necessity for recreation and for hauling fire wood. These Acadians built ice boats out of a simple arrangement of wooden-cross-members on steel runners, with a mast and sail. Smaller ones were used for fun and larger ones could be used for transporting heavy loads, such as fire wood, across the ponds or on the sea ice.

Acadians also had homemade horse-drawn sleighs and carriages, which were sometimes used for taxis, but mostly for riding to and from church or other special events. Wagons that were used for hauling wood and hay might also be used for carting herring and capelin. A mixture of fish was a fertilizer for their crops. There was always a blacksmith or two who could make horseshoes, pitch forks, cart wheels and wheel-rims for wheelbarrows, some of the basics needed on the farm.

These talented pioneers also built their fish sheds on the beaches. They built wooden skids to launch their homemade row dories and wooden capstans to haul them up. (Capstan- an upright drum around which cables are wound to haul in something heavy that is attached to the cable, like an anchor, dory, boat etc.) The Acadians became experts at making anchors, called kellicks that were made of a heavy rock encased in wood. These men and women skillfully handcrafted their own lobster pots that they ballasted with beach rocks. Likewise, they knitted their own nets for fishing salmon, cod and herring, with wooden netting needles that they again, diligently made. Finally, to make sinkers for the nets, the Acadians poured hot lead into molds.

Kippens Namesake

In 1836, a gentleman by the name of Benjamin Kippen married Frances Bagg. The married couple lived near Romaines and the river that runs through that area came to be known as Kippens River, after Benjamin Kippen. Benjamin was a ship builder and in 1837 he built a schooner in honor of his daughter, who was twenty-one years old at the time. He named his schooner, Elizabeth, after her. The ship was constructed at the river; it weighed sixteen tons and was thirty-eight feet long. Around the same year, John Bagg, a brother to Frances Bagg above, married a woman named Hannah. In the early 1840s, John and Hannah moved to Port aux Basques. Benjamin and Frances also moved and settled in Burnt Islands.

Last Farm in Kippens

It was their attachment to the land that first drew Acadian pioneers to the Stephenville area. As early as the mid 1800s their skills as farmers allowed them to flourish into a bountiful community. Before the American Base in 1941, those French pastoral settlers, Constance Aucoin among them, populated the 'Indian Head' or 'Back of the Pond' area, as well as plots of arable land, in and around Stephenville and beyond. One of the most important things about the area was the availability of water, which was a necessary asset to the Americans in the 1940s. There were plenty of brooks and ponds and the whole area was situated over one large aquifer. The Americans found out, as had the Acadians before them, that they only had to dig down 25 or 30 feet to find water. They sustained themselves well, off this Utopia, in their 'Paradise of the North', as Americans once labelled it.

JE SUIS JACKATAR – SEQUEL TO BACK OF THE POND

Below is an excerpt from a document[41] that was written by an American teacher, Mrs. Claxton Ray (née Gay Cotney), wife of an American officer. Mrs. Ray wrote of her experiences, after she came to Harmon Field, in the summer of 1953. Just two years later, her husband resigned his commission in the United States and his family returned as Canadian citizens to live in Newfoundland. Mrs. Claxton Ray wrote as follows:

"Newfoundland has the greatest hunting and fishing in the world[42]: salmon, cod, trout, flounder, lobster, seal, black bear, moose, caribou, and duck, all within a twenty-five-mile range of Stephenville." The winters are really nice here and "farming sections produce some fabulous[43] vegetables, twenty-five-pound heads of cabbage, two-foot-long carrots, Irish potatoes weighing six pounds and strawberries as large as peaches. Hey! I didn't say it, she did. And to even think that I believed, that my dad, Paddy Benoit, was exaggerating all those years.

To once again quote Misty MacDonald and Heather Thistle in their 1998 article on Acadian Village, "Stephenville was actually established because of poverty and strife existing in Nova Scotia and the excellent fishing grounds and farm land that this community had to offer." In fact, these Acadian pioneers, who made 'Back of the Pond' their home, were direct descendants of those affected by the great upheaval, the Expulsion of 1755 out of Acadia.[44]

After 1941, and the need to set up an Air Force Base in Stephenville, Newfoundland, all liviers were asked to leave their properties and their homes and resettle elsewhere. Once again, uprooting seemed part of their destiny: they must find property on which they could build a new home, property suitable for growing crops and raising livestock. They must face a daunting task of rebuilding their lives. Most were devastated and lonely, once they left; by moving they had lost their sense of community.

---

[41] Mercedes Benoit-Penney, *Back of the Pond 1ˢᵗ Ed*. 2017, P193 – 197
[42] Mercedes Benoit-Penney, *Back of the Pond 1ˢᵗ Ed*. 2017, P195
[43] Mercedes Benoit-Penney, *Back of the Pond 1ˢᵗ Ed*. 2017, P197
[44] Mercedes Benoit-Penney, *Back of the Pond 1ˢᵗ Ed*. 2017, P197

JE SUIS JACKATAR – SEQUEL TO BACK OF THE POND

Unlike American bases on our East Coast, those Acadian farmers had to leave their livelihoods. Their jobs had been to sustain themselves by fishing, planting and growing their own crops, thus supplying food for themselves and their animals. It was a full-time job, but one that was very rewarding to these Catholic families with their Mi'kmaq ties. **The expropriation was necessary in order to make room for an American Base, which was established to assist its allies in the war efforts of World War II.**

Some settled in Codroy Valley, where soil was rich with minerals and nutrients; others searched out farm land in Cold Brook, Kippens, in and around Stephenville and elsewhere. My grand-father, James Benoit, for instance, grew root crops behind our home on West Street; in a field we called "Grandpa's Back Field." Crops were so healthy, that the Americans decided to make use of still existing rich farm land that the liviers had to vacate. Mr. James Jollimore was hired by the Americans to oversee the growth of root vegetables and corn for mess halls[45]. In fact, the Americans didn't cease operation of that farmland until 1955. With the arrival of Ernest Harmon Air Force Base came hundreds, maybe thousands of jobs and newcomers.

The temptation of employment, with its monetary gains, drew some further away from their farms and brought an influx of people to the area. Still, some could not detach themselves from the good soil. Municipalities became more regulated and farms were seen as a nuisance, with noises and odours. Some citizens then decided, if you had an animal that meows or bow-wows, you're an animal lover and well received; but if your animal moos, oinks or clucks, you're a menace to society.

In recent times, there was an issue with the last farm in Kippens. Gerald and Cora Aucoin, descendants of Constance Aucoin, still have a self-sustaining farm that's been in the family since 1895. In light of the growth in housing, the community of Kippens has become more regulated. Sadly, the Kippens Council had ordered the Aucoin couple

---

[45] Mercedes Benoit-Penney, *Back of the Pond 1st. Ed.* 2017, P 118

to remove fencing, signage, livestock buildings and livestock from their property, but, thank goodness, have since rescinded the order.

Hopefully, we never close the door on the last chapter of our legacy. We need to preserve our history, not destroy it. If this were a building, we would be proud to display it as a heritage place, enticing tourists to our beautiful community, home of Paralympic athlete, Katarina Roxon, who won gold in the 100-metre breaststroke. The Aucoin farm should be seen for the precious gift it is, to the people of Kippens.

New costly Federal legislation requires farms to change the way they grade eggs, forcing West Coast egg farmers out of business. In past years, the Newfoundland farmers prepared and graded their own eggs. Today, however, those jobs have been conveniently handed over, by government, to Newfoundland Egg Inc., situated where, you ask? Would you like to take a guess? Of course, nothing ever changes!

New legislation forces egg farmers to send all eggs to Roaches Line where they are graded, washed and packed, creating numerous jobs for the eastern part of the Island. Then the eggs are trucked across the Trans Canada Highway for the second time, to be sold in Newfoundland or the rest of Canada. Newfoundland Egg Inc. has the capacity to grade eggs for the entire province and doubts whether there will ever be a need for a grading station in Western Newfoundland again.

Well, of course, we didn't expect any better here on the Southwest Coast. Let me reiterate what Right Reverent Father Sears learned in the 1860s and still prevails today. "Spending money on our coast is like throwing money away," right? Government, provincial and federal, have a way of sucking the economic life blood from the rural communities.

JE SUIS JACKATAR – SEQUEL TO BACK OF THE POND

Ingenuity

We, on the Southwest Coast of the Island, have such a unique advantage because of our location. One noticeable practice of deviation from the truck system was that of fishermen in St. Georges, back in the early 1900s. These men would saw ice blocks out of nearby ponds in springtime and store them in sawdust cellars that they built. Sawdust was used as insulation, keeping the ice blocks from melting. So, in May, June and July these fishermen caught salmon early in the morning, processed them as was needed and stored them in these cellars.

They also built crates that could be filled with ice and salmon and could be carried by two men. They then transported these crates of salmon to the nearby railway station, via horse and cart. In the evening, when the train arrived, the crates would be put on the passenger train, for their destination, a number of stops across the Island going east. Salmon was also prepared in the same manner for the Gulf Ferry to North Sydney.

In keeping with the exact time of the train routes and the Gulf Ferry runs, fish were transported overnight to docks in Nova Scotia. The fish had now entered a different country altogether, Canada. (Remember, this was before Newfoundland entered Confederation in 1949.) Further processing, if required, was made and the fish would normally reach its market that same day. These were Jackatars in progress.

Winter Houses

The use of winter houses was a common practice by the pioneers. You have to remember that most of the homesteads were built along the coastline, because of the fishery, which was the primary resource of income. Those summer residences in Sandy Point did not have protection from the cold winter winds, and there was little wood close by. In fact, firewood needed to be hauled to that settlement. A second residence, with lots of firewood, in a sheltered area, was in most cases necessary and was referred to as the winter house. Subsistence farming might require land, in yet another location, for crops and for pasture. So sometimes, even a temporary third residence might be found:

(1) On the Western coastal area of the Port au Port Peninsula. The winter houses were located about halfway between Lourdes and Black Duck Brook. These houses were built among the trees, not far from the coast. The sign for Winterhouses still identifies the community.

(2) In Stephenville and/or Barachois Brook wooded areas, just in from the coast.

(3) In the Three Rivers area, at inland shelters, on the St. David's roadway.

Major Design Flaw

In at least one notable instance, a resourceful Jackatar in Kippens decided to have both his winter house and his summer home under one roof, but completely partitioned across in the middle. The winter house was on the eastern or leeward side, because of the prevailing westerly winds. The summer home was on the windward side and acted as a barrier in winter against colder, prevailing westerly winds. Entry doors and windows on the summer home were larger, for (solar gain). The winter house had a smaller entry door and smaller windows (less heat loss). Travel time to and from the summer and winter homes was practically nil! Duh! What do I mean practically nil! They had to pack up everything they needed for the season and carry it all the way from one end of the house to the other. Come to think of it, there was a major design flaw.

There should have been a door inside, in the middle partition, don't you agree? So, I wonder, does this make this ingenious Jackatar as stun as he looks? Hey, nobody's perfect. I'm sure Frank Lloyd Wright, the famed architect, would have been impressed by the ingenuity of the design. It should be noted that in that era, entry door measurements were not standard size, even to the point that you might identify the home owner by the height and width of his door. Sometimes, dimension could be even smaller, depending on how frugal the homeowner was.

Entry Door – approximately 4 feet

Introduction of Coal

Winters were cold and sometimes long, and firewood was the only source of heat. Waking up to a cold house was the norm. There had to be a better way. When coal was first introduced to the area, it was considered a major breakthrough. Before that, the firewood would burn out during the early morning hours and required further tending, which was seldom done. Thus, 'it was cold and lonely in the deep dark night, but they could seek Paradise by the Kerosene light'.

In 1947, an enterprising resident, Mr. Patrick White of St. George's, purchased a used Canadian Navy patrol boat. These crafts were available at bargain prices and were economical to operate. Since coal was readily available, a short distance away, in Cape Breton, Mr. White began a coal delivery service to St. George's Bay. Because of the introduction of coal, there was a concern that the fertility rate might drop and alter the demographics. However, this fear proved unfounded.

JE SUIS JACKATAR – SEQUEL TO BACK OF THE POND

Toot, toot, here comes the choo-choo train! The westbound freight train would arrive in the early hours of the morning and wake up many of the residents, with the clatter of the rails and other noises of the steam engine. The adults, now wake and alert, realized it was too early to get up and too late to go back to sleep. Thus, the number of pregnancies remained stabilized. For some, that train became affectionately known as the 'See-Alice Special'.

The last run of the "Newfie Bullet"- 1969

'Yes, Sir! They could hear that train a-comin', a-rollin round the bend. That train not only inspired our Acadian ancestors to make babies, it also inspired Johnny Cash to write his classic song, 'Folsom Prison Blues'.

<u>Folsom Prison Blues</u>

I hear that train a comin', a-rollin' round the bend
I ain't seen the sunshine, since I don't know when
I'm locked in Folsom Prison, and time keeps draggin' on
And I hear that train a-rollin', on down to San Antone

When I was just a baby, my mama told me "Son,
Always be a good boy, don't ever play with guns"
But I shot a man in Reno, just to watch him die
When I hear that lonesome whistle, I hang my head and cry

I bet there's rich folks eatin', in a fancy dining car
They're probably drinkin' coffee and smokin' big cigars
Well, I know I had it comin', I know I can't be free
But I hear that train a-rollin' and that's what tortures me

Well, if they freed me from this prison and that railroad train was mine
I bet I'd move it on, a little further down the line
Far from Folsom Prison, that's where I long to stay
And let that train keep a-rollin' and roll my blues away

JE SUIS JACKATAR – SEQUEL TO BACK OF THE POND

Stride and Eastman

I remember the name Stride from my father's days. He used the name often, when he spoke of his hunting and fishing trips. Dad also guided many an interested party in search of the big rack, or the largest catch (fish). When he told of his experiences in the wilderness, he was also known to spin a tale or two, like the following: He told us of a married couple from Stephenville (Back of the Pond), in the 1930s, who didn't have much, and so they worked out a plan. Every time they had sex, they would put twenty-five cents in the piggy bank and save up to buy something special. Five years later, they had a chance to buy a second-hand car, so the husband said "I'll go see how much we have saved up and we can try to get a loan for the rest." When he opened the piggy bank, it was full of ten and twenty dollar bills. "Now, how in the hell did that get there", asked the husband. His wife answered "Well, you know, not everyone is as stingy as you."

In Picture #1 the man on the right is Benjamin (Ben) Stride, Mi'kmaw, sometimes known as Ben Strait. He was born in Conne River, Newfoundland, in the year 1896. He died at Black Duck Siding in 1962 and is buried in Stephenville Crossing in the old cemetery. He spent a great deal of time in Bay St. George. He had a lucrative job as a guide in Newfoundland, one that the Mi'kmaq were experienced at.

The other man in the picture has been described as Mr. Kodak. If the identification is correct, the person referred to would be George Eastman, Inventor of the Kodak Camera. George Eastman, (Mr. Kodak) a high school dropout, was born in

Left – Right: George Eastman (Mr. Kodak), Ben Stride (Mi'Kmaw Guide)
Picture #1

Rochester, New York in 1854. He was an only son and never married. He became an entrepreneur and a philanthropist, after he founded the Eastman Kodak Company. As a result, rolls of film became commercialized and anyone could practice the art of photography.

In 1906, in his early 50s, Eastman came to Newfoundland. As an outdoorsman, he camped, fished and hunted. One of the destinations that Eastman was believed to have frequented and photographed, was that of the Bay St. George area. In 1910, he visited Labrador, where he accumulated a second collection of images of the wild and rugged country, while enjoying the pleasures of sport related activities. Two separate albums, both held within the 'Legacy Collection' at George Eastman House, in Rochester, were compiled exclusively to hold the images of those two trips.

Eastman is said to have donated one hundred million dollars to charities, an immense fortune by today's standards. He was an avid fisherman and hunter but it is also possible that the person in the photo, if not Eastman himself, maybe one of the high ranking officials of the Kodak Company.

While visiting Newfoundland, Eastman used the services of guides to travel the wilderness. He had the following picture taken on one of those excursions. It is believed that Mi'kmaw trapper, Ben Stride, may be among them. This photograph was taken with or by the rich and famous Mr. Kodak. The fact that Eastman was so far away from his home in the United States, taking pictures of Mi'kmaq guides in Newfoundland, highlights the importance of Ben Stride and other Mi'kmaq guides and shows their ingenuity. Eastman was very fond of Harry's River in Black Duck Siding. This farming and forestry community, east of Stephenville is renowned for its Atlantic salmon.

The Guides – George Eastman House Legacy Collection
Picture #2

JE SUIS JACKATAR – SEQUEL TO BACK OF THE POND

Southwest Region Cabot Committee
Researched and written by Donald Gale

Emile Benoit – Master Fiddler
Ingenuity

"Ta da da dee dum, Ta da da dee dum sang Emile as he sat on his bed and pretended to play the violin, using one stick for a bow and another for a fiddle. He kept time, with both wool stocking feet on the wooden floor and moved his head from side to side so that his whole body moved in time to the music. There was no danger of anyone downstairs hearing him and coming up to tell him to go to sleep. There was a party going on at Amedie Benoit's house and with two violins going and four men step dancing, the bit of noise Emile made could not be heard by anyone.

The men playing the violins were his uncle, John Duffenais, who lived next door, in the village of Black Duck Brook, and a Mr. MacInnis from the Highlands. Mr. MacInnis and the other men, came to Black Duck Brook on the Port au Port Peninsula, every Spring, to fish for lobsters. When they came to Newfoundland, the Highlanders brought their violins and played Scottish tunes. Emile liked nothing better than to listen to these jigs, reels and strathspeys, (a type of dance tune), as well as to traditional French tunes played by his uncle and a few other men of the area.

Emile dreamed of playing for people to dance with his own violin. He would not ask his parents, Amedie and Adeline, to buy him one, because money was too scarce to waste on violins for little boys. This was in the early part of the century and people all over Newfoundland were poor. Emile, however, admired his uncle John and thought that he could do just about anything, so one day he asked him to make a violin for him. To Emile's surprise and delight, his uncle said "yes."

People worked long and hard in those days and there was not a lot of time, especially in summer, for unnecessary tasks, such as violin making. There were fish to catch and dry, hay to cut, lobsters to catch and deliver to the cannery, cows to milk, crops to weed, and a thousand other things to do, just to survive.

The weeks passed by and every time Emile saw his uncle, he asked him about the violin. His uncle did not get angry or impatient, as some people would, but always said, "by and by, when I get time." Eventually, Emile grew tired of asking and gave it up. He tried to make his own violin by stretching pieces of thread across a small wooden box, with holes on the top, but could get no sound from it. He did realize, that with the addition of a sound post, a small peg fitted between the top and bottom of the box, he would have been able to produce sounds, much like a real violin.

One day that fall, long after Emile had given up hope, his uncle showed up with a brown paper package under his arm. "Here", he said to Emile, "try this." Emile took the package and found it surprisingly light. He was scared to open it at first, scared that it would not be his violin, but something else. He was sure his uncle had forgotten the promise he had made. With trembling hands Emile untied the string and unwrapped the present. He could hardly believe his eyes; there it was. It was made of dark brown wood and shaped just like the ones the older men played. There was a bow, filled with real hair from a horse's tail and a little piece of rosin, that Emile knew, had to be rubbed on the bow, before you could make music.

Emile was so surprised, he forgot to say thank you. He held the instrument carefully, by the neck and plucked the strings. He rubbed some rosin on the bow and drew it lightly across the strings, just above the bridge. The sound that came out, may not have been a note on the scale, but to Emile it was the most beautiful sound in the world.

"Here", he said to his uncle. "Play me a tune", so his uncle played a tune, a jig that Emile recognized as a favourite of the Highland players. He watched where his uncle put his fingers on the strings, along the neck of the violin and how he see-sawed the bow back and forth, touching sometimes one string, sometimes two or more. When his uncle finished the tune, Emile said "play the first part again." His uncle did so, and Emile watched very carefully. "Here, you try it", his Uncle John said. But Emile did not want to. Instead, he took the instrument to his room and began to practice and experiment.

The next time his uncle came to visit, Emile took out the violin and proudly played the tune for him. It was not perfect, but amazingly good for someone with no training and only a few days practice. In his teens, Emile had realized his dream and was in great demand to play for square dances and at weddings and parties.

As Emile's family got older, he found more time to play his music and travel. He once travelled to Louisiana and played with Cajun musicians. These are people descended from the Acadian French who were expelled from their homes in what is now Nova Scotia, by the British, in the 1700s. They speak French, as did Emile, and he enjoyed his time down there.

On another occasion Emile was invited to Saint-Malo, in France, where his ancestors had come from. Besides being an excellent fiddler, Emile composed hundreds of tunes about local people and places, such as 'Piccadilly Slant', and 'Diane's Happiness'. Once, he even named a tune 'Bandsaw Reel' to mimic the sound of a bandsaw. 'Emile's Dream', was one that he dreamed about. He woke up humming the tune, and having no tape recorder, called his sister to record it over the telephone. His sister, Mary Felix, recalls the night very well, and says she was happy to do it for him.

Emile's music has been recorded on tape and CD and is available at most music stores. Musicians, such as Kelly Russell, were influenced by Emile. One young, popular traditional musician is Emile's nephew, Bernard Felix, son of the lady who did the telephone recording. Bernard plays the accordion and is recognized as a master of that instrument.

JE SUIS JACKATAR – SEQUEL TO BACK OF THE POND

Louis Phal

First known as Louis Phal and anglicized as Louis Fall, African Legend Boxer, 'Battling Siki', received his nickname 'Siki' at an early age. The nickname, which has native and colonial connotations, stuck with him throughout his short life.

Poor and illiterate, Siki, in his youth, grew up in a crime filled part of West Africa, during very turbulent times. He was born in Saint Louis, Senegal, in 1897 and died at the age of 28, on the West Side of Manhattan, N.Y. Returning home to his drab apartment in the early morning hours, he was shot in the back with two .38 caliber bullets. The setting for his death was aptly named 'Hell's Kitchen', because of its dim and sinister gutter qualities.

On September 4, 1922, over 55,000 people showed up to watch the fight between Siki and the already celebrated Frenchman, George Carpentier, who owned the title, 'Heavyweight Champion of Europe'. Siki, Lois Phal, was declared winner by a knockout and was awarded the 'Light Heavyweight Championship of the World.'

Meantime, back here in Bay St. George, we also had what legends are made of, our Jackatar friend, Richard Bennett (Benoit, b. 1910 d. 1965), who equally loved the sport of boxing, as well as marathon running. Thus the same nickname 'Siki' was bestowed on him by the locals. They realized that it was an appropriate name for someone who could defy the odds. So, in 1934, we find Richard travelling by train to Grand Falls and taking part in a marathon, a long-distance running race. In doing so, he surprised the judges, beating out the other contestants. That qualified him for the 1934 British Commonwealth Games that were being held in London, England. His name, Siki, quickly came to be known by sports enthusiasts, both locally and throughout the colony.

At an early age, Siki had worked in the lumber woods with his father at Little Barachois Brook and South Brook. In his adolescence he had moved to Grand Falls where he was introduced to the art of Boxing by Mike Shallow, who soon became his coach. Siki had a successful boxing career and had the good fortune to be associated with other notable boxers such as Jimmy Pond, Joe Byrne, Art Pomeroy, Al Dwyer and Curtis MacDonald.

Regularly, a pulp and paper shipment travelled to London, England, from the Grand Falls Mill. The local mill officials made arrangements for Siki to travel to the United Kingdom on one of their vessels, ensuring his participation in the 1934 Commonwealth games. Thus, a Mi'kmaw hopeful, competed, but failed to place in the tops ranks. The Legend, however, had begun.

'Fighting Siki' returned from that voyage across the 'Big Pond' (the Atlantic Ocean) on the S.S. Emilie Maersk. Siki tells in thrilling detail of his fight with the Lightweight Champion of England at Swansie and of the knockout blow given him in the sixth round.

Siki had given up going to sea. He claimed that the sea gave a fellow weak legs, so he then intended to stick to Terra Firma (solid ground) where he could deliver that knockout to the solar plexes in jig time. He died an untimely death at the age of 55 on February 5, 1964. Siki Bennett showed great interest in the youth of the area. Through hard work and dedication, he was able to share his coaching abilities. Many people in St. George's are much better off today, because they had Siki Bennett as a mentor.

Jigg's Dinner

People on our Southwest Coast were never used to having things handed over to them. In the past, I reiterate, what others took for granted, our rural communities had to make for themselves. As a result, past generations continued to be inventive.

One good example, of an invention, that comes to mind, was given to my husband, as a gift. I'll give the device a name; let's call it a jimmy, because it fits the dictionary definition

Jimmy

so well. The fact that it was also made by a man whose name is Jimmy, just spices up my narrative.

Maybe not immediately obvious by the photo, this crowbar of sorts, the jimmy, is a useful device to help open the traditional buckets of salt beef[46] that Newfoundlanders have come to love so much. From inside that bucket comes the salt beef that is the  highlight of our famous 'Jigg's Dinner'. In addition to being the main course of the dinner, salt beef is often cooked on Sundays, as well. It gives flavour to the vegetables, when the main course is something other than the salt beef i.e. chicken, turkey etc.

The tradition of salting beef goes back to the 20th Century, before freezers, when the beef would spoil rather quickly, if it were not salted. The salt greatly increased the life span of the product.

If you are thinking that the beef bucket outgrew its usefulness after the Jigg's Dinner, you would be dead wrong. Just as important to the livelihood and diet of most Newfoundlanders are the wild berries. Come summer and early fall months, it is a common practice and traditional for hundreds of Newfoundlanders, of all ages, to go berry picking. Clad in waterproof footwear, scarves, suntan lotion and/or fly dope they can be found with empty beef buckets in hand, heading into the bush. Quads, cars and trucks line up, most any dry day in the summer months, along our gravel roads, while their owners chase after the elusive wild berries. Such delicacies vary from blueberries, partridgeberries to the less plentiful strawberries, raspberries, squash berries, bakeapples and other varieties not mentioned.

So, here's to the salt beef buckets; they've gotten me out of more than one pickle. And, last but not least, hats off to the beef producers and the makers of the salt beef buckets. From my young childhood

---

[46] https://www.facebook.com> *Chalkers* **Salt Meat**

days of picking berries with my parents, to this day, I have yet to witness a handle breaking on one of those buckets. After a long hot day picking, the last thing you want is to spill your bucket of berries on your way back to your vehicle, or before you have a chance to get the cover on.

More than once, over the years, I've turned to the internet to enquire about how to patent an invention. I've learned that doing so is very expensive, time consuming and very seldom worth pursuing. That's too bad, because I'm aware of a tool that has the potential of saving lives among our young skidooers and snowmobilers. Without a patent, creative ideas, like Jimmy's, go to waste.

Chapter 9

Hockey

Alchamadyk – Hurley or Hockey on Ice

The Greek philosopher Plato, student of Socrates, teacher of Aristotle, was the founder of philosophical writings, written around 380 B. C. (before Christ) in ancient Greece. Although the true author is unknown, Plato himself used the proverb '<u>necessity is the mother of invention</u>'[47] in his translations of 'Plato's Republic', which means, roughly, that when the need for something becomes imperative, we are forced to find ways to achieve or invent it.

As the saying goes, necessity surely was, and is, the mother of invention. Before the age of technology and industrialization, the Mi'kmaq created their own pastime and invented, out of necessity, what they needed. If they needed to get across bodies of water quickly, for instance, to hunt, to cut wood or to connect with friends and family, walking the perimeter took too much of their time. So, for spring and summer seasons, when the ice was melted on the ponds, the Mi'kmaq built canoes, from birch bark, to carry them over to the other side. In wintertime, when the ponds were frozen over and the land was snowbound, walking any distance could be treacherous and very time consuming. These nomadic inventors had to make, not only their shoes or mukluks, but also snowshoes, in order to be able to traverse the ponds and the snowbound terrain. The only roads they had were the animal trodden paths, or those they beat down themselves, so the snowshoes were a necessity for hunting, walking or even some sport related activities. Still, the snowshoes, although buoyant on snow covered terrain, weren't at all suitable for crossing windswept and/or frozen ponds or lakes. So, once again, the Mi'kmaq built sleds, with metal runners, that could he hauled by horse across

---

[47] www.dictionary.com *Necessity is the mother of invention.*

the ice, in the frozen months. These sleds could be used to transport firewood, caribou, moose or other kill that they depended on, year around, for their many needs.

To perform other tasks, though, like ice fishing or skating, the Mi'kmaq would wear their mukluks, or strap a homemade rudimentary form of skate onto their footwear. Since ice skating was a frequent pastime, it wasn't unusual for the Mi'kmaq to adopt a game like Hurley and adapt it into the game of ice hockey. Hurley was played on the ice with a stick and a ball, and was common in Ireland's Gaelic community way back in the 1700s. The stick that was used to play the game, was similar to the hockey stick used by the Mi'kmaq, but not identical. In Hurley, the ball actually balances on the blade of the Hurley stick, while in hockey; the puck is slid across the ice by the stick. In 1920, the shape of the Hurley stick-blade was made shorter and wider, to accommodate the balancing of the ball and this shape has been retained up until today. Hurley sticks are traditionally carved out of the ash tree.

Montreal, Qc. or Kingston, Ont. would like to believe that the game of hockey originated in their city and province. They have to concede, though, that as far back at the 18th century (the early 1700s) the Mi'kmaq of Nova Scotia were playing hockey on the frozen ponds. These Indigenous had their self carved sticks, homemade skates, wooden pucks and game rules that they perfected, long before the game was introduced to other provinces.

With little technology, in that day, the hockey stick was not even marketed until 1860, after which time the game of ice hockey started to flourish in other parts of Canada. It was in that same year that the sticks for the game of hockey, carrying the brand 'Mic Mac', began to sell nationally and internationally from the Starr Manufacturing Company in Dartmouth, Nova Scotia. Colonial histories record that Canadian cities like Montreal and Toronto purchased those Mic Mac sticks and used the same game rules that were originally perfected in Nova Scotia. The sticks were made locally, on reserves, such as Shubenacadie and the Annapolis Valley native communities. In fact, in 2006, a stick made by the Mi'kmaq in the 1850s, at the time the oldest known, was sold at an auction for $2.2 million; it had been appraised in the United States for $4.25 million.[48]

There is proof, by documents and oral history that the Mi'kmaq carved their sticks from the hornbeam trees around 1890, at around the same time the sport became popular in Canada. The Dartmouth Mi'kmaq carved out sticks, with the use of a crooked knife, which they also made by hand. They created a one-piece ironwood stick, from the ironwood or hornbeam tree, sometimes referred to as stinkwood, because of its fowl odor, when it was cut in two. When supplies of hornbeam trees started to diminish, because of the large demand for the sticks, the Mi'kmaq used the yellow birch tree, because it had the same strong qualities as the hornbeam. So, to sum up, in addition to the Mic Mac hockey sticks, the rules of the game, the wooden pucks, even the Starr hockey skates, all originated with the Mi'kmaq Indians in Nova Scotia. Other contributions to the game, by Nova Scotia in later years, were the hockey net, the position of rover and the forward pass.

There is little doubt that the evolution of hockey, here in South-Western Newfoundland, came about as a result of migration from Nova Scotia. It was inevitable, with the arrival of the French Acadians and their Mi'kmaq friends and family members that the sport is played here, on our ponds and homemade rinks. 'Homemade rinks were still commonplace, when I was a child growing up in the 1950s.'

---

[48] https://www.the globe and mail.com/sports/Hockey-stick-billed-as oldest-ever-nets $2.2 million/article///2379/)the Globe and Mail (Revised April 7) 2009

JE SUIS JACKATAR – SEQUEL TO BACK OF THE POND

Organized Hockey

The first records of organized hockey here on the Southwest Coast, that I am able to find, date back to the 1960s. In 1969/70, Western Star Sports Editor, Richie Williams, wrote the following:
(All information is credited to him, as it was reported.)

Top attraction in Bay St. George area
1968 - 1969

Hockey was unorganized in the Bay St. George area, as little as four years ago, but today it has blossomed into the area's top sports attraction.

The conversion of an airplane hangar into the beautiful Stephenville Gardens, three years ago, started the ball rolling and the sport has been growing in popularity since.

Hockey is in an ideal situation in Bay St. George. There's a great rivalry between centres entered in the league – St. George's, Port au Port, Stephenville Crossing and Stephenville – and this makes for great fan interest

The 1968-69 hockey season has to be the best yet, for officials connected with all aspects of the game.

Bay St. George has a sound minor hockey system, with over 700 boys participating and the senior loop just ended its third straight successful campaign.

The senior loop was very competitive, with the final games of the regular season schedule, giving the Stephenville Monarchs first place honors, over the Stephenville Crossing Rangers. The arch rivals met again in the playoffs and the Monarchs came out on top in seven games.

It was the Monarchs first year in the league. Last season Stephenville had two teams entered, but the town's officials decided to combine the two clubs this year.

About 15,000 fans watched the finals between the Monarchs and Rangers, an average of over 2,000 fans per game.

Bay St. George has been very successful in provincial intermediate 'B' play. They finished second behind the Clarenville Caribous both years, for the Newfoundland title.

The season was pleasing for senior league president, George Hutchings. "It was a very successful year – financially and otherwise." Hutchings said Wednesday.

"Our local league operated well. We had good fan support and the Monarchs could have won the intermediate 'B' title, except for injuries to a couple of key players."

Juniors, 1968 -1969

Bay St. George's next step in Newfoundland hockey may be in the Junior Division.

A possible entry into the Newfoundland Amateur Hockey Association Senior Division would undoubtedly kill fan interest in the local league, whereas fans would tend to support the area's representatives in provincial play.

But officials feel Bay St. George could support a good junior setup, since about 50 per cent of the senior league is comprised of junior-aged players.

"This is going to be a big step for us next year," Hutchings said, "we thought about the possibilities of junior hockey last season and we're going to get it off the ground."

The Bay St. George league plans to operate a junior league with at least two teams. However, it is hoped enough players are on hand to have one team from each centre.

"We have no plans of seeking entry into NAHA senior. That would be the worst thing we could do." Hutchings pointed out.

Plans for future years call for a coach for the Bay St. George area.

"We're hoping that if industries get developed here, we will probably be looking towards Corner Brook, for some of the older players, who are ready to throw in the towel."

"We don't want him as a hired coach. He will get employment in the town and coach the players. That's what we need, a few experienced guys, who can pass along their knowledge to the other players."

Hutchings was high in his praise for Hector Caines, former star with the Corner Brook Royals and the Buchans Miners in NAHA competition. "There's no way in the world to give Hector too much praise. He helped the Monarchs, but the kids on the other teams watched him and learned an awful lot," he said.

Hutchings looks forward to a better year next season. "Hope to have an improved calibre of hockey and I think it will be more competitive in all four centres."

The genial president said the league is striving to balance out the teams.

With the addition of a junior league, "We will make sure all players and juniors coming up, will be skating and participating in a league," Hutchings said.

The senior league will hold its annual banquet and presentation of trophies May 10.

George Faulkner, Manager Coach of the Corner Brook Royals, said that "Newfoundland teams tended to bring in, from the Mainland, inferior players and coaches, players not as good as some of the locals. He added that there were scores of top-notched hockey players in Newfoundland, but the potential had never been tapped." He felt fortunate to represent Canada and Newfoundland on the National Team. Faulkner made those remarks as guest speaker at the League's annual banquet and presentation of trophies, for the Bay St. George Hockey League, at the Harmon Base School.

JE SUIS JACKATAR – SEQUEL TO BACK OF THE POND

In the four-team league, St. Joseph's High School, St. George's, captured six of the seven awards that were up for grabs. They won the league and playoff titles, while Greg Bennett was awarded the most 'gentlemanly player trophy'; Jerry Stride won the 'most valuable and top scorer'; Howard Skinner was 'best goaltender' and Ben Goodyear of Stephenville Amalgamated got 'best defenseman.'
By Richie Williams, Western Star Sport Editor, 1969

Jackie Doucette

Again, in 1969/70, the Western Star reported the following 'Newfoundland Player Inks[49] with Quebec Player,' as follows:

Jackie Doucette, native to Newfoundland has been inked by the 'Quebec Cornwall Royals' to the 1969/70 Hockey team. From Aguathuna, NL, a six-foot, 175 pounds, Jackie played center and was 18 years old at the time.

Jackie played three seasons with Port au Port in the Atlantic Senior Hockey League. In that last season, he established a scoring record with 44 goals in 18 games. He also had 16 assists.

I understand that Jackie Doucette, the scoring star of the Bay St. George Hockey League last season, is doing pretty well with the Cornwall Royals of the Quebec Junior Hockey League.

Doucette to date has scored something like eight goals in four exhibition games. This isn't at all bad, for a fellow who has only a couple of years of organized hockey under his belt.

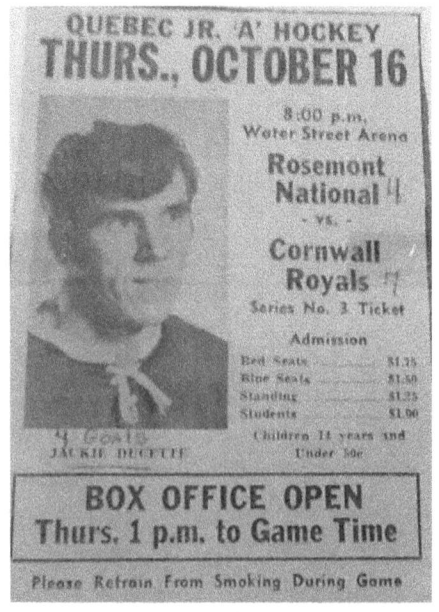

[49] Signed a Contract

JE SUIS JACKATAR – SEQUEL TO BACK OF THE POND

Jackie played with the following lineup in the Quebec Junior A Hockey League, Cornwall Royals 1969 – 1970, Eastern Division.

William Smith
Robert Houlihan
Keith Maiden
Michel Ruest
Michel Boivenue
Marc Landry
Paul Ross
Michel LeRoux
Jim Munch
Pierre Lascelle

Barry Brooks
Larry Salmon (collarbone)
George Rodney
Jackie Doucette**
Michel Renaud
Claude Fraser
Garry Herrington
Dennis Roy
Gerald Campeau

Coach: Jim Larin
Trainer: Yvon LeMire
Manager: Norm Baril

JE SUIS JACKATAR – SEQUEL TO BACK OF THE POND

Bay St. George Senior Playoff Champions
1968 – 1969

Tuesday night, the Stephenville Monarchs captured the playoff title in the Bay St. George Senior Hockey League, with a 5-2 victory over the Stephenville Crossing Rangers.

Members of the team kneeling:
L - R: Jim Kennedy, Al Sewell, Ron Hayden, John Alexander, Ross Black, Walter Crotty.

Standing:
L – R: Hector Caines, Jack Tilly (Trainer), Bob Burroughs, Ted MacWhirter, John Parsons, Eric Goodyear, Wayne Gaultois, Al Comeau, Ian Benard, Ben Goodyear, Bern Young, Gord Hiscock (Assistant Coach), Wayne Collicott and Larry Smith (Matthews photo)

Bay St. George Hockey League award winners 1968 – 1969

Hockey Players in the Bay St. George League this season, who captured the prized silverware, display their trophies, during the league's annual banquet, held at Riverside Casino on Saturday night.

Front Row L – R: Gary Mercer of the Crossing Rangers; Ross Black, holding the League and Playoff Championship Trophies (for the Monarchs) and Fred Wells of the Crossing Rangers

Back Row L - R: Melvin Bennett of the Rangers; Lloyd Messervey of the Athletics; Howard Skinner of the Athletics and Hector Caines of the Monarchs.

Missing from picture are Jackie Doucette and Hayward Lucas.
(Woolridge Photo)

JE SUIS JACKATAR – SEQUEL TO BACK OF THE POND

Bay St. George High School Hockey League 1968 – 1969

Players in the Bay St. George High School Hockey League received trophies during the league's annual banquet and dance, held in Stephenville on Friday night.

L – R: Fred Pye, Danny Connolly, Howard Skinner, George Faulkner, Ben Goodyear, Greg Bennett and Jerry Stride.

George Faulker, Manager-Coach of the Corner Brook Royals was the banquet's guest speaker.

All players with the exception of Goodyear played for St. Joseph's High School, St. George's. (Star Photo)

JE SUIS JACKATAR – SEQUEL TO BACK OF THE POND

Bay St. George Hockey League Receive Awards 1969 – 1970

Players winning awards, in the Bay St. George Senior Hockey League last season, were presented with their trophies at the league's annual dance, held last week.

Award winners L – R: Hector Caines, most goals, most assists and top scorer; John Alexander and Glen Newhook, top goaltenders; Heber Noel, president of the champions Stephenville Monarchs and Amedius Hynes, best defenseman.

Standing L – R: George Power, rookie-of-the-year; Melvin Bennett, most gentlemanly player; Lloyd Messervey, coach of the year; Dave Kean, most valuable player and George Hutchings, league president. (Photo by Gibbons)

JE SUIS JACKATAR – SEQUEL TO BACK OF THE POND

Port au Port Vikings 1970 – 1971

L - R Back Row: John Joe McCann, Ed Hawco, Tony Ulino, Jamie Keating, Len Barter (Goalie), Mike McIntosh, Graham Smith, Jerry Gaudon, Jackie Doucette, Pat Hawco, Stan Doucette.

L – R Front Row: Art Butt, Ed Nosewothy, Harold Kerr, Wayne Meade, Glenn Newhook, Junior Hawco, Brian or Roger Jesso

JE SUIS JACKATAR – SEQUEL TO BACK OF THE POND

League and playoff champions
Port au Port Vikings 1971 – 1972

Port au Port Vikings climaxed a fine season in the Bay St. George Hockey League Sunday afternoon, after capturing the playoff title, by sweeping the finals in four games against St. George's Athletics. The Vikings also finished in first place in regular season play.

Team members are:
Back row L – R: Junior Hawco, Art Butt, Ben Goodyear, Graham Smith, Steve Cormier, Kevin Pilgrim, Harold Kerr, Wayne Hounsell, Jackie Doucette and Leonard Barter.

Front row L - R: Ed Noseworthy, Mike McIntosh, Billy Hynes, Glenn Newhook, Alex Hawco and Del Keating. (Star photo)

JE SUIS JACKATAR – SEQUEL TO BACK OF THE POND

Intermediate B Champions (1970 – 1972)

Bay St. George Huskies whipped Goose Bay in two straight games during the weekend to capture the provincial Intermediate B Hockey title at Stephenville Gardens. It marked the first time the Huskies won the provincial crown. They lost out to the Clarenville Caribous in the finals in each of the three previous years. (Chappell photo)

Huskies Selected

The Bay St. George League released the names of players who will make up the Bay St. George Huskies and the Junior Huskies for provincial play.

Players to try out for the Senior Huskies were selected by Jamie Keating, Coach of the League Champion Port au Port Vikings. Keating will handle the Huskies.

Players selected are: Wayne Hounsell, Graham Smith, Junior Hawco, Jackie Doucette, Brian Goodyear and Mike McIntosh of the Vikings, Amedius Hynes of the Rangers, Cal Gillingham, Len Blanchard, Vince White, Frank Deveroux, Roy Kavli and Max Ollerhead of St. Georges Athletics and Dave Dawe, Art Barry, Jim Kennedy, John Alexander, John Parsons and Guy McLaughlin of the Monarchs.

The Junior Huskies will be made up of the following players: Danny Connolly, Greg Cutler, Jimmy Bennett, Kevin Pilgrim, Del Keating, Len Barter, Harold Kerr, Derek Styles, Alvin Smith, Steve Cormier, Clarence Casey, Myron Gallant, Randy White, John Hutchings, Dave Murphy, Gerald Hall, Eugene Mercer, Wayne Power and Glen Newhook. The players were selected by Coach Hector Caines and it is hoped to arrange a couple of exhibition games for the Juniors, before they start play in the all Newfoundland Junior 'A' league, later this month. The team got off to a good start last week when they beat the Bay St. George Midget All Stars 5 -1.

The league stressed that players can be dropped or others picked up at any time and this is not necessarily the final makeup of the teams.

JE SUIS JACKATAR – SEQUEL TO BACK OF THE POND

The Stephenville Monarchs
Circa 1972 – 1974

The Stephenville Monarchs captured the playoff championship in the Bay St. George Hockey League, Sunday afternoon with a 4-0 win over the Port au Port Vikings. The Monarchs, at one point in the series, were down 2–0, but roared back with four straight victories, to win the best of seven finals.
(Unfortunately, the names of the above team members are not available)
(Star Photo)

JE SUIS JACKATAR – SEQUEL TO BACK OF THE POND

PEE WEE CHAMPIONS

Circa 1970s

Bay St. George took top honours in the Pee Wee Championship match, all Newfoundland Section B, which was played at the Harbour Grace Stadium Saturday, April 17.

Shown front L – R Randell LeSaga, Manuel McIsaac, Phil March, Ricky Swyers, Keith Styles, Terry Styles, Tony Duffenais (Captain), Bob Lambe, Joey Corbett and Hilario Rodriguez.

Back row L – R Kevin Stacey, Irv Mackie (Manager), Ray Mullins, Kennie Bruce, Randy McIsaac, Gordon Piercey, Gus Willette (Coach), Wendell Russell, Calvin Alexander and Gary Morgan. The trophy was presented to the lucky team by Brian Wakelin
(Max Mercer Photo)

JE SUIS JACKATAR – SEQUEL TO BACK OF THE POND

Unorganized Hockey

Father Joy's Memorial High 1963 – 1965

This picture was taken in front of Father Joy's Memorial High School, a former convent in Port au Port West, next to the biggest wooden church in Newfoundland and Labrador, 'Our Lady of Mercy.'

Front L – R: Harold Keough, Hal Compagnon, Junior Hawco, Dave Penney

Back L – R: Noel Kelley, Gus Marche, Joe House, Bill Penney, Bill Duffy, Mike Gushue.

Missing: Conrad Glasgow, Wayne Lee, Abbie Alexander.

This hockey team, "Father Joy's Memorial High," was together for approximately four years, losing only one game, while playing local teams in the Bay St. George area.

JE SUIS JACKATAR – SEQUEL TO BACK OF THE POND

Chapter 10

Memories - are made of this

By Arthur W. F. Barrett

Later this year, 2016, the town of Stephenville will be celebrating the 50th anniversary of the closing of Ernest Harmon Air Force Base. This has inspired me to jot down a few memories of my association with Stephenville and surrounding area – particularly the Base. I'm delighted that the Town Council is marking this occasion, as the American Base was the mainstay of that area's economy, for many years.

My memory of 'Harmon' is clear in my mind, but my memory of the area goes back quite a few years before that, and I would like to share those memories with you.

As a young boy in the 1930s, my family from Curling and two Goodyear families from Grand Falls, used to spend part of our summers in Stephenville Crossing. I always considered it our summer holidays, I soon learned that father wanted to go salmon fishing on Harry's River.

For a few years, we all stayed at Bishop's Hotel. It was a wonderful place and the bishops were kind and over-generous folk. There were two sons in the family that I remember well (much older than I). Bob, who had a vintage touring car, would take us on all-day excursions to Stephenville, Port au Port, and Aguathuna, always stopping in Stephenville on the return journey, to purchase strawberries from the fields of businessman A.V. Gallant. Those strawberry fields were located where Ernest Harmon Air Force Base was later constructed. Their other son was Syd, who owned a bicycle and would lend it to me, once in awhile. That made my day!

In later years, Syd's daughter married former Premier and former Chief Justice, and my personal friend, Clyde Wells.

JE SUIS JACKATAR – SEQUEL TO BACK OF THE POND

During those hazy lazy days of summer, I became quite friendly with one of the Goodyear daughters, Jean. Jean was a nice girl, about my age, and used to sing 'Red Sails in the Sunset,' to me. I think it was what one would call, 'puppy love.' We all spent hours on the beach (which now has a highway running right across it), or exploring the sand dunes at Gut Bridge, or picking bakeapples, in the area known then as the Butter Factory, – all the joys of youth.

After Bishop's Hotel burnt down, our place of abode became McFatridge's Hotel, which served our needs and was quite comfortable.

One year, as a teenager, I was at the Crossing on my own, attending a Junior Forest Warden's Camp, on the grounds of the old cabin. One day myself and a friend Gussy Young (a Crossing resident), were detailed to go to A. V. Gallant's store (about a ¼ mile) to purchase a stone (14 pounds) of flour. We took turns carrying the bag of flour 'til Gussy had the bright idea that if we cut the bag in two we would only have to carry seven pounds each! Producing a pocket knife, he soon had the bag divided. We arrived back at camp with considerably less flour than the 14 pounds bought and paid for! We had a sports day at the end of the camp, and that's when I became champion pole vaulter.

In 1942, I accepted a summer job with the Newfoundland Base Contractors, an American firm engaged to build Harmon Field, as it was then known. I worked in the personnel department processing the paper work when someone got hired. I had an American counterpart and we worked together doing the same job, only he was paid three times my salary! Note: (The Americans were willing to pay equally for Newfoundland workers. However, our British Officials in St. John's feared, that if workers on the Bases got more pay than the staff of business owners in St. John's, they would probably lose the staff or, they might have to pay their workers higher wages. Negotiations for land, homes and work at Harmon Base etc. were taken out of the hands of the Americans and into British hands, with very unfavourable results.) That point is still being argued today –

equal pay for equal work. Dr. O'Connell, my next door neighbour in Curling, had a son, Charlie (same age), who also had a summer job at Harmon that year – he was a grease monkey, having to apply grease to all the heavy equipment. Charlie went on to become a famous surgeon, and as I write, now lives in retirement in Kitchener, Ontario.

At Harmon, I was billeted in a building located in an area called 'Skunk Hollow'. Why it was called that I have no idea – it was fine, clean and comfortable.

There was only one 'watering hole' in Stephenville in those days – a tavern owned by Morris Boland of Curling. I remember that establishment well. Not that I consumed much beer, but because of two young ladies who worked there. They were sisters who had come from Deer Lake. I can't remember their first names, but I believe their last name was Oats/Oake. They were lovely, good-looking girls, and every time I ventured inside, the older of two would play 'Yours' on the juke box, and dance with me. She was a marvellous dancer and such a nice person. I've thought of those two girls often, down through the years, and I know that if they married and had children, they would have made wonderful mothers.

House parties, or 'kitchen parties' as they are commonly known, were numerous in those days, and I was privileged to be invited to quite a number of homes such as the Abbotts, the Joys and the Gillis's.

In 1957, I found myself back in Stephenville once again, but this time as the CBC Management Representative at the American Base Television Station. It came about this way: The Americans wanted to establish one of their armed forces television stations on the Base, which was their policy worldwide, but Canadian law prohibits foreign nationals from holding a broadcast license in Canada. However, a deal was struck between the American Embassy in Ottawa and the C.B.C. whereby the C.B.C. would apply for a license to establish a television station at Ernest Harmon Air Force Base, to be managed by the C.B.C. but having American Air Force personnel as operators. Quite a unique situation! It was then that I felt I had joined the Diplomatic Corps.

We rented a lovely home on West Street, situated between St. Stephen's Cemetery and the R.C.M.P. Headquarters – a real quiet neighbourhood!

My job was not without problems, but nothing that couldn't be resolved. The American had granted me a shadow rank of 'Field Grade Officer', which meant that I had the same rank as any officer over the rank of Major. So, I was on an equal footing with the Base Commander and the Wing Commander, Mrs. Goyt. This made it much easier to resolve problems that arose from time to time, such as 'Why do we have to play God Save the Queen at sign-off?'

My office was located in the Base Command Headquarters – just down the hall from the Base Commander. On Friday, November 22nd, 1963, I was sitting in my office, and the teletype machine that was used for receiving news items from C.B.C. St. John's (and personal messages to me), started up, and I crossed the room to see what was being received. It was a news item of the assassination of President Kennedy. I took the item off the machine and proceeded up the hall to the Base Commander's office. I asked if he was aware of this news, and he wasn't. While he was reading the item, I noticed he pressed a button on the side of his desk and within seconds, two C.I.A. agents arrived at the door. They escorted me back to my office; one stood guard over my teletype and the other at my office door. Within minutes, the Base was placed on full alert.

I had been issued a pass that simply stated that I was 'sterile', which meant that I could move freely around the base and was excused from all alerts. It is just a coincidence that we never had any more children after that pass was issued.

JE SUIS JACKATAR – SEQUEL TO BACK OF THE POND

Elvis Presley

One evening, I was sitting at home, when I received a phone call from an American colleague, advising that Elvis Presley would be arriving at the MATS (Military Air Transport Service) terminal in about an hour; he was returning to the U.S. from his army assignment in Germany. I wasn't overly excited, but I knew my teenage daughter, who was an Elvis fan, would be over the moon to actually meet the 'King.' She had retired for the night, but when I woke her with the news, she was up and dressed, before I got downstairs. Her meeting with Elvis late that night, must have impressed her, because on her 40th anniversary, she and her husband traveled to Las Vegas and were remarried in the Elvis Chapel by a very skinny, 'Elvis.'

There were many exciting events during my years at Harmon. The 4th of July was always fun, with lobster boils and amusements. On the 1st of July, 1963, (Canada Day) the United States Air Force acrobatic team – the Thunderbirds performed a wonderful show in the sky over Stephenville.

Then there was the official opening of the new Officer's Club. It was on May 9th (the year escapes me at the moment) and it was a black-tie event. The Americans spared no expense, and had brought in entertainers from the U.S. Highlighting the entertainers were the Strolling Strings from Washington, D.C.

A hostess had been brought in from Montreal. She was very good-looking and appeared to be very efficient. However, she didn't last long and we all wondered why. We didn't have to wait long. Her name made headlines from London all around the world – a political scandal. Who remembers Christine Keeler and the Profumo affair? This was a political scandal, brought on by a sexual affair of a 19 year old model and the Secretary of State, in 1961.

The years I spent in Stephenville were enjoyable and rewarding. I became the first President of the Rotary Club, and organized and became the first Commanding Officer of 708 Stephenville Squadron, Royal Canadian Air Cadets, and at one time was Chairman of the

Amalgamated School Board. My two children attended school in Stephenville – my son started kindergarten the same year my daughter started grade eleven, and they would go off each morning hand in hand.

I have nothing but pleasant memories of the years spent in and around the Stephenville area. When I spent time at the Crossing as a teenager, I had a friend by the name of Ron O'Keefe. He served his country with honour and distinction during the 2nd World War and married a war bride – Barbara. My late wife was also a war bride and a Barbara. Both Barbara's came to Newfoundland in 1946, on the same ship, the SS Drottingholm. The two Barbara's have now gone, but they both left their mark on Newfoundland and the lives of Newfoundlanders.

I'm sure many people have some wonderful memories connected with the 50th anniversary of the closing of Ernest Harmon Air Force Base, and I hope they will share them with the Stephenville Town Council, leading up to the anniversary month.

Arthur W. F. Barrett
9 Madigan Place
Empire Village
St. John's, NL AIE 6B4

JE SUIS JACKATAR – SEQUEL TO BACK OF THE POND

Arthur Barrett
B. 1924, D. May 9, 2019

NOTE: The two-story house, once owned by the CBC and lived in by Mr. Barrett, is still standing, near the East end of the Roman Catholic cemetery.

The family of Arthur Barrett was deeply saddened by his recent passing in St. John's, NL at the age of 95. He was predeceased by his wife Barbara Bettine (Micklethwaite). Arthur retired in 1983, following a 37 year career with the Canadian Broadcasting Corporation. Beginning, in 1946, as a broadcaster, he held several senior management positions and retired as Regional Manager of Administrative Services for the Newfoundland and Labrador CBC Region.

Arthur was a veteran of World War II, a member of the Royal Canadian Air Force Bomber Command and a life member of the Bomber Command Organization. Equally as important were his roles as a member of the Air Force Association of Canada, the Royal Air Force Officer's Club (London, UK), and he served on numerous boards. His other service organizations included Rotary, Lions International, the Atlantic Symphony, the Dominion Drama Festival, the Yorkshire Air Museum, the Newfoundland and Labrador Drama Society and the National Multicultural Theatre Association. He will be lovingly remembered by all who knew him, as a highly organized, humorous and extremely kind and giving individual.

(1) It has been proven over the centuries that this area has a natural attraction for a variety of cultures. Bay St. George offered a sanctuary from an oppressive class system back in European Society.

(2) Another of its attractions was its endless acres of fertile land, fresh-water streams and lakes. All was complemented by an abundance of flora and fauna.

(3) Even pirates found their haven behind Sandy Point. In fact, the further one travelled into the Bay, the closer they came to their own Acadie.

Bibliography

Benoit-Penney, Mercedes. *Back of the Pond*, Revised Edition, 2018, page 75

Butt, Kirk R. *The Inner Bay, page 447, 448*

Day, John *Canadian Historical Review, Vol 38.* Under the Newfoundland & Labrador Heritage Website

Dictionary, Webster. *https://merriam-webster.com/dictionary - rascal.*

Dictionary of Newfoundland English

Fergusson, C. B. *Cabot's Landfall,* https://dalspace,library.dal.ca 1954

Heritage, Newfoundland and Labrador. *The Recent Indians of the Island of Newfoundland*

Hanrahan, Maura Ph.D *"The Lasting Breach..The Omission of Aboriginal People from the Terms of Union between Newfoundland and Labrador and Canada and its ongoing Impacts",*

Hillier, James & Higgins, Genny, updated Website Project. *Cape Breton Landfall Argument 1997 Newfoundland and Labrador Heritage*

House, Jerome. "My Aguathuna "One Mile Square"." In *My Aguathuna "One Mile Square"*, by Jerome House, 171. St. John's: DRC Publishing, 2013.

https://commons.wikimedia.org.wiki

https://www.historyextra.com. *A Brief History of the Vikings.* November 26, 2018

https://www.penguinandrandomhouse.ca.

Morris, Don St. John's. "West Coast Mines Held Promise." *Vignettes of the West*, Unknown.

Native author's view / history of the Vatican Wampum Belt
http://tribes.tribe.net/realdealhistory/thread/

Reisman, Jonathan. The Fight For The Right To Eat Seal Blubber *https://slate.com>2017/10>the fight.* October 9, 2017

Urban Dictionary.com

www.appmanalee.com/pinterest

www.stockfreeimages.com

Acknowledgements

Thank you to the many people, who helped me along the way including:

Barrett, Arthur (Posthumously)
Benoit, Albert & Leslie
Bourgeois, Francis
Cuff, Harry
Doucette, Carleen
Doucette, Ursie
Eddy, Reg
Gale, Donald
Gale, Frank
Gallant, Bernice (Posthumously)
Gallant, James/Jimm
Harvey, Bev
LeRoux, Raymond
Madore, Aaron & Family of Ronald Madore
Marche, Pat
Mercer, Bob
Muise, Leonard
O'Quinn, Mary
Pilgrim, Bill
Pretty, Lloyd (Posthumously)
Saunders, Harley
Schumph, Ursula
White, Theresa
Young, Aiden

Merci!

Thank you to Ursula Schumph, who played a dual role, typing and editing, as we went through the difficult process of preparing this book for print. Thank you for being so supportive, never giving up on me, even in the face of my endless revisions. It was a pleasure working with you. Instead of being hard work, you made the experience seem like fun. I am honored to call you and Ray my friends. All the best!

JE SUIS JACKATAR - SEQUEL TO BACK OF THE POND

Our Family

Penneys

Bill · Mercedes

Cameron · Bobby (Son) · Sheryl · William

Burtons

Landen · Jadeyn · Dawn (Daughter) & Kent · Hudson · Ashlyn

Flavens

Jonah · Laura (Daughter) · Donovan · Jonathan · Lucas

About the Author

Mercedes Benoit-Penney was born, raised and educated in Stephenville. She graduated with a Bachelor of Arts/Ed. Degree from Memorial University. As a teacher and mother, she advocated for educational standards in the local school system and wrote editorials for newspapers and magazines.

Mercedes began writing during her school days for therapeutic reasons, which developed into a passion in later years to record the ancestry of her Acadian background. She is now retired and devoting more time to music as well as researching the diverse culture of the area.

Her earlier books, Back of the Pond, Original and Revised, have become a source of historical reference for cultural heritage groups of the region. One such group is that of the Stephenville Historical French Culture Association, Incorporated July 23, 2019. Members are welcome by contacting Clyde Russell email gullpondnl@hotmail.com

Historic, French Cultural Association Inc.

Association Culturelle Francaise Historique de Stephenville Inc.

On July 23, 2019, the Stephenville Historic French Cultural Association was consolidated under the Incorporations Act of Newfoundland and Labrador.

The Corporation's mission is to establish a central focal point for the historical record of the French language and culture that existed in the Bay St. George area, prior to the establishment of Ernest Harmon Air Force Base.

The Corporation's vision is to establish an authentic French cultural site (near the old hospital). The site would contain the history of the community and families prior to 1941. It would also serve as an annual tourist attraction and educational resource for schools in the area.

Objectives are:

(1) To promote the revival of the French language and culture in the Stephenville, Bay St. George area.

(2) To research, record and maintain the historical record of the francophone families and community in the Stephenville area prior to 1941.

(3) To construct and maintain traditional French, a Newfoundland 1940s era house and farm works on acreage close to the original settlement. The corporation is a non-profit organization.

JE SUIS JACKATAR - SEQUEL TO BACK OF THE POND

Life's Like That

I'd like to share one more item with you before I go. I have to confess, computers are not exactly my forte. I am more of the old school, paper and pencil type. Where computers offer most people relaxation, a place to alleviate anxiety, they do the opposite for me. Finally, after much contemplation, though, I agreed to take some Facebook Computer lessons from my sister-in-law, Leslie. She patiently walked me through the motions of connecting with friends etc. until I stopped hyperventilating and could manage to accept and reply to a message.

I thought I was doing really well. Proud of my accomplishments, I arrived home one day anxious to tell my husband, Bill, all about my new computer skill. More than that, I wanted to tell him about a friend of ours, whom I had connected with on Facebook. We hadn't heard from him in a long time and all I could recall was that his wife had died and he had moved away with his children. I was surprised but thrilled to find him on Facebook. I couldn't recall his name, but we passed friendly messages back and forth. He asked how Bill was and we agreed not to be such strangers in the future.

Anyway, to get back to Bill, I filled him in on the details, all about my experience that I was so proud of. I felt so elated, on a bit of a high, I guess. When I finally finished, Bill was looking at me really hard. I will never forget what he said "Merc (short for Mercedes)! So and so has been dead for 5 years. It was his wife who went away to live with her children. So, who in the hell were you talking to?"

A Dream

One night, I woke up from my sleep to have this message racing through my mind, I ran for a paper and pencil before I'd forget the following: Boys, don't let your testicles grow up to be obstacles.

JE SUIS JACKATAR - SEQUEL TO BACK OF THE POND

Pictures to share

If anyone with a picture of John Thomas Alexander and would be willing to share the same, please contact either Austin Alexander or Marie Alexander at the following phone numbers 709-643-4385, 709-643-5567 or 709-214-1231.

If anyone has a picture of Thomas White (LeBlanc) born March 9, 1878 and died 1940 and would be willing to share the same, please contact Mercedes Benoit-Penney at 709-648-9561 or by email billpenney47@gmail.com.

Note: More books to follow on the Early History and French Acadian/Mi'Kmaq theme.

P.S. Can you (young-at-heart) find the dinosaur in one of the chapters?

Notes